CONTENTS

CONTACT LIST

You know you're a horse person when
you start clucking at people to move.

Use this Contact List as both a directory for your clients and as a reference guide to locate their Horse and Client Information Sheet by filling in the page number that their record appears on.

NAME	ADDRESS	EMAIL	PHONE	PAGE #

NAME	ADDRESS	EMAIL	PHONE	PAGE #

NAME	ADDRESS	EMAIL	PHONE	PAGE #

NAME	ADDRESS	EMAIL	PHONE	PAGE #

NAME	ADDRESS	EMAIL	PHONE	PAGE #

NAME	ADDRESS	EMAIL	PHONE	PAGE #

NAME	ADDRESS	EMAIL	PHONE	PAGE #

NAME	ADDRESS	EMAIL	PHONE	PAGE #

BOOKKEEPING

It always has been and always will be
the same in the world: the horse does
the work and the coachman is tipped.

CASHFLOW SHEETS

DATE	DESCRIPTION	INCOME	TRUCK / EQUIPMENT	GAS	TOOLS / SUPPLIES	PHONE	TAXES, FEES INSURANCE	HEALTH EXP.	INCIDENTALS EG. REPAIRS	FORM OF PAYMENT
	DETAILS	CASH IN				CASH OUT				

CASHFLOW SHEETS

	DETAILS		CASH IN	CASH OUT							
DATE	DESCRIPTION		INCOME	TRUCK / EQUIPMENT	GAS	TOOLS / SUPPLIES	PHONE	TAXES, FEES INSURANCE	HEALTH EXP.	INCIDENTALS EG. REPAIRS	FORM OF PAYMENT

CASHFLOW SHEETS

	DETAILS	CASH IN	CASH OUT							
DATE	DESCRIPTION	INCOME	TRUCK / EQUIPMENT	GAS	TOOLS / SUPPLIES	PHONE	TAXES, FEES INSURANCE	HEALTH EXP.	INCIDENTALS EG. REPAIRS	FORM OF PAYMENT

CASHFLOW SHEETS

	DETAILS	CASH IN	CASH OUT							
DATE	DESCRIPTION	INCOME	TRUCK / EQUIPMENT	GAS	TOOLS / SUPPLIES	PHONE	TAXES, FEES INSURANCE	HEALTH EXP.	INCIDENTALS EG. REPAIRS	FORM OF PAYMENT

CASHFLOW SHEETS

DATE	DESCRIPTION	INCOME	TRUCK / EQUIPMENT	GAS	TOOLS / SUPPLIES	PHONE	TAXES, FEES INSURANCE	HEALTH EXP.	INCIDENTALS EG. REPAIRS	FORM OF PAYMENT
	DETAILS	**CASH IN**				**CASH OUT**				

CASHFLOW SHEETS

	DETAILS		CASH IN	CASH OUT							
DATE	DESCRIPTION		INCOME	TRUCK / EQUIPMENT	GAS	TOOLS / SUPPLIES	PHONE	TAXES, FEES INSURANCE	HEALTH EXP.	INCIDENTALS EG. REPAIRS	FORM OF PAYMENT

CASHFLOW SHEETS

| DATE | DESCRIPTION | CASH IN | CASH OUT | | | | | | | |
		INCOME	TRUCK / EQUIPMENT	GAS	TOOLS / SUPPLIES	PHONE	TAXES, FEES INSURANCE	HEALTH EXP.	INCIDENTALS EG. REPAIRS	FORM OF PAYMENT

CASHFLOW SHEETS

	DETAILS		CASH IN	CASH OUT							
DATE	DESCRIPTION		INCOME	TRUCK / EQUIPMENT	GAS	TOOLS / SUPPLIES	PHONE	TAXES, FEES INSURANCE	HEALTH EXP.	INCIDENTALS EG. REPAIRS	FORM OF PAYMENT

CASHFLOW SHEETS

| DATE | DESCRIPTION | CASH IN | | | CASH OUT | | | | | |
		INCOME	TRUCK / EQUIPMENT	GAS	TOOLS / SUPPLIES	PHONE	TAXES, FEES INSURANCE	HEALTH EXP.	INCIDENTALS EG. REPAIRS	FORM OF PAYMENT

CASHFLOW SHEETS

DATE	DESCRIPTION	INCOME	TRUCK / EQUIPMENT	GAS	TOOLS / SUPPLIES	PHONE	TAXES, FEES INSURANCE	HEALTH EXP.	INCIDENTALS EG. REPAIRS	FORM OF PAYMENT
	DETAILS	CASH IN	CASH OUT							

CASHFLOW SHEETS

| DATE | DESCRIPTION | CASH IN |||||||| FORM OF PAYMENT |
		INCOME	TRUCK / EQUIPMENT	GAS	TOOLS / SUPPLIES	PHONE	TAXES, FEES INSURANCE	HEALTH EXP.	INCIDENTALS EG. REPAIRS	

CASHFLOW SHEETS

DATE	DESCRIPTION	INCOME	TRUCK / EQUIPMENT	GAS	TOOLS / SUPPLIES	PHONE	TAXES, FEES INSURANCE	HEALTH EXP.	INCIDENTALS EG. REPAIRS	FORM OF PAYMENT
	DETAILS	CASH IN				CASH OUT				

CASHFLOW SHEETS

DATE	DESCRIPTION	CASH IN								
		INCOME	TRUCK / EQUIPMENT	GAS	TOOLS / SUPPLIES	PHONE	TAXES, FEES INSURANCE	HEALTH EXP.	INCIDENTALS EG. REPAIRS	FORM OF PAYMENT

CASHFLOW SHEETS

DATE	DESCRIPTION	INCOME	TRUCK / EQUIPMENT	GAS	TOOLS / SUPPLIES	PHONE	TAXES, FEES INSURANCE	HEALTH EXP.	INCIDENTALS EG. REPAIRS	FORM OF PAYMENT
	DETAILS	CASH IN			CASH OUT					

CASHFLOW SHEETS

DATE	DESCRIPTION	INCOME	TRUCK / EQUIPMENT	GAS	TOOLS / SUPPLIES	PHONE	TAXES, FEES INSURANCE	HEALTH EXP.	INCIDENTALS EG. REPAIRS	FORM OF PAYMENT
	DETAILS	CASH IN	CASH OUT							

CASHFLOW SHEETS

DATE	DESCRIPTION	INCOME	TRUCK / EQUIPMENT	GAS	TOOLS / SUPPLIES	PHONE	TAXES, FEES INSURANCE	HEALTH EXP.	INCIDENTALS EG. REPAIRS	FORM OF PAYMENT
DETAILS		**CASH IN**		**CASH OUT**						

CASHFLOW SHEETS

DATE	DESCRIPTION	INCOME	TRUCK / EQUIPMENT	GAS	TOOLS / SUPPLIES	PHONE	TAXES, FEES INSURANCE	HEALTH EXP.	INCIDENTALS EG. REPAIRS	FORM OF PAYMENT
	DETAILS	CASH IN				CASH OUT				

CASHFLOW SHEETS

DETAILS		CASH IN	CASH OUT							
DATE	DESCRIPTION	INCOME	TRUCK / EQUIPMENT	GAS	TOOLS / SUPPLIES	PHONE	TAXES, FEES INSURANCE	HEALTH EXP.	INCIDENTALS EG. REPAIRS	FORM OF PAYMENT

CASHFLOW SHEETS

	DETAILS	CASH IN	CASH OUT							
DATE	DESCRIPTION	INCOME	TRUCK / EQUIPMENT	GAS	TOOLS / SUPPLIES	PHONE	TAXES, FEES INSURANCE	HEALTH EXP.	INCIDENTALS EG. REPAIRS	FORM OF PAYMENT

CASHFLOW SHEETS

	DETAILS	CASH IN	CASH OUT							
DATE	DESCRIPTION	INCOME	TRUCK / EQUIPMENT	GAS	TOOLS / SUPPLIES	PHONE	TAXES, FEES INSURANCE	HEALTH EXP.	INCIDENTALS EG. REPAIRS	FORM OF PAYMENT

CASHFLOW SHEETS

DATE	DESCRIPTION	INCOME	TRUCK / EQUIPMENT	GAS	TOOLS / SUPPLIES	PHONE	TAXES, FEES INSURANCE	HEALTH EXP.	INCIDENTALS EG. REPAIRS	FORM OF PAYMENT
DETAILS		**CASH IN**	**CASH OUT**							

ANNUAL ACCOUNT SUMMARY (Year: _____)

	Jan	Feb	Mar	Apr	May	Jun	Jul	Aug	Sept	Oct	Nov	Dec	TOTAL
Income													
Expenses													
Net Income													

EXPENSES

	Jan	Feb	Mar	Apr	May	Jun	Jul	Aug	Sept	Oct	Nov	Dec	TOTAL
Gas													
Insurance													
Phone													
Vehicle Payments													
Equipment Payments													
Tools													
Supplies													
Vehicle Repairs													
Equipment Repairs													
Taxes													
Bank Fees													
Health Expenses													
Ass'n Dues													
Other Prof'l Costs													
Business Lunches													
Clinics and Education													
Incidentals													
TOTAL													

ANNUAL ACCOUNT SUMMARY (Year: _____)

	Jan	Feb	Mar	Apr	May	Jun	Jul	Aug	Sept	Oct	Nov	Dec	TOTAL
Income													
Expenses													
Net Income													
EXPENSES													
Gas													
Insurance													
Phone													
Vehicle Payments													
Equipment Payments													
Tools													
Supplies													
Vehicle Repairs													
Equipment Repairs													
Taxes													
Bank Fees													
Health Expenses													
Ass'n Dues													
Other Prof'l Costs													
Business Lunches													
Clinics and Education													
Incidentals													
TOTAL													

ANNUAL ACCOUNT SUMMARY (Year: _____)

	Jan	Feb	Mar	Apr	May	Jun	Jul	Aug	Sept	Oct	Nov	Dec	TOTAL
Income													
Expenses													
Net Income													

EXPENSES													
Gas													
Insurance													
Phone													
Vehicle Payments													
Equipment Payments													
Tools													
Supplies													
Vehicle Repairs													
Equipment Repairs													
Taxes													
Bank Fees													
Health Expenses													
Ass'n Dues													
Other Prof'l Costs													
Business Lunches													
Clinics and Education													
Incidentals													
TOTAL													

HORSE AND CLIENT INFORMATION SHEETS

Your horse's behavior always seems to depend
on the number of people watching you

CLIENT INFORMATION	Name:				
	Address:				
	Phone:		Email:		

HORSE INFORMATION	Name:		Breed:		
	Gender:		Primary Use:		
	Age:		Temperament (1-10):		

Veterinarian:	HOOF ANGLES			HOOF LENGTHS		
		Left	Right		Left	Right
Trainer:	Front			Front		
	Back			Back		

Health Concerns:	Supplements:	Shoe Size:
		Shoe Type:
		Shoe Pads:
Therapeutic Treatments:	Special Requirements:	Dates Due:
Notes (Problems, Consultations, Changes, etc.):		Stable Name / Address:

CLIENT INFORMATION	Name:				
	Address:				
	Phone:		Email:		

HORSE INFORMATION	Name:		Breed:		
	Gender:		Primary Use:		
	Age:		Temperament (1-10):		

Veterinarian:	HOOF ANGLES			HOOF LENGTHS		
		Left	Right		Left	Right
Trainer:	Front			Front		
	Back			Back		

Health Concerns:	Supplements:	Shoe Size:
		Shoe Type:
		Shoe Pads:
Therapeutic Treatments:	Special Requirements:	Dates Due:
Notes (Problems, Consultations, Changes, etc.):		Stable Name / Address:

CLIENT INFORMATION	Name:						
	Address:						
	Phone:			Email:			
HORSE INFORMATION	Name:			Breed:			
	Gender:			Primary Use:			
	Age:			Temperament (1-10):			

Veterinarian:	HOOF ANGLES			HOOF LENGTHS		
		Left	Right		Left	Right
Trainer:	Front			Front		
	Back			Back		

Health Concerns:	Supplements:	Shoe Size:
		Shoe Type:
		Shoe Pads:
Therapeutic Treatments:	Special Requirements:	Dates Due:
Notes (Problems, Consultations, Changes, etc.):		Stable Name / Address:

CLIENT INFORMATION	Name:						
	Address:						
	Phone:			Email:			
HORSE INFORMATION	Name:			Breed:			
	Gender:			Primary Use:			
	Age:			Temperament (1-10):			

Veterinarian:	HOOF ANGLES			HOOF LENGTHS		
		Left	Right		Left	Right
Trainer:	Front			Front		
	Back			Back		

Health Concerns:	Supplements:	Shoe Size:
		Shoe Type:
		Shoe Pads:
Therapeutic Treatments:	Special Requirements:	Dates Due:
Notes (Problems, Consultations, Changes, etc.):		Stable Name / Address:

CLIENT INFORMATION	Name:		
	Address:		
	Phone:	Email:	

HORSE INFORMATION	Name:	Breed:
	Gender:	Primary Use:
	Age:	Temperament (1-10):

Veterinarian:	HOOF ANGLES			HOOF LENGTHS		
		Left	Right		Left	Right
Trainer:	Front			Front		
	Back			Back		

Health Concerns:	Supplements:	Shoe Size:
		Shoe Type:
		Shoe Pads:
Therapeutic Treatments:	Special Requirements:	Dates Due:

Notes (Problems, Consultations, Changes, etc.):	Stable Name / Address:

CLIENT INFORMATION	Name:		
	Address:		
	Phone:	Email:	

HORSE INFORMATION	Name:	Breed:
	Gender:	Primary Use:
	Age:	Temperament (1-10):

Veterinarian:	HOOF ANGLES			HOOF LENGTHS		
		Left	Right		Left	Right
Trainer:	Front			Front		
	Back			Back		

Health Concerns:	Supplements:	Shoe Size:
		Shoe Type:
		Shoe Pads:
Therapeutic Treatments:	Special Requirements:	Dates Due:

Notes (Problems, Consultations, Changes, etc.):	Stable Name / Address:

CLIENT INFORMATION	Name:						
	Address:						
	Phone:			Email:			
HORSE INFORMATION	Name:			Breed:			
	Gender:			Primary Use:			
	Age:			Temperament (1-10):			

Veterinarian:	HOOF ANGLES			HOOF LENGTHS		
		Left	Right		Left	Right
Trainer:	Front			Front		
	Back			Back		
Health Concerns:	Supplements:			Shoe Size:		
				Shoe Type:		
				Shoe Pads:		
Therapeutic Treatments:	Special Requirements:			Dates Due:		
Notes (Problems, Consultations, Changes, etc.):				Stable Name / Address:		

CLIENT INFORMATION	Name:						
	Address:						
	Phone:			Email:			
HORSE INFORMATION	Name:			Breed:			
	Gender:			Primary Use:			
	Age:			Temperament (1-10):			

Veterinarian:	HOOF ANGLES			HOOF LENGTHS		
		Left	Right		Left	Right
Trainer:	Front			Front		
	Back			Back		
Health Concerns:	Supplements:			Shoe Size:		
				Shoe Type:		
				Shoe Pads:		
Therapeutic Treatments:	Special Requirements:			Dates Due:		
Notes (Problems, Consultations, Changes, etc.):				Stable Name / Address:		

CLIENT INFORMATION	Name:	
	Address:	
	Phone:	Email:
HORSE INFORMATION	Name:	Breed:
	Gender:	Primary Use:
	Age:	Temperament (1-10):

Veterinarian:	HOOF ANGLES			HOOF LENGTHS		
		Left	Right		Left	Right
Trainer:	Front			Front		
	Back			Back		
Health Concerns:	Supplements:			Shoe Size:		
				Shoe Type:		
				Shoe Pads:		
Therapeutic Treatments:	Special Requirements:			Dates Due:		
Notes (Problems, Consultations, Changes, etc.):				Stable Name / Address:		

CLIENT INFORMATION	Name:	
	Address:	
	Phone:	Email:
HORSE INFORMATION	Name:	Breed:
	Gender:	Primary Use:
	Age:	Temperament (1-10):

Veterinarian:	HOOF ANGLES			HOOF LENGTHS		
		Left	Right		Left	Right
Trainer:	Front			Front		
	Back			Back		
Health Concerns:	Supplements:			Shoe Size:		
				Shoe Type:		
				Shoe Pads:		
Therapeutic Treatments:	Special Requirements:			Dates Due:		
Notes (Problems, Consultations, Changes, etc.):				Stable Name / Address:		

CLIENT INFORMATION	Name:		
	Address:		
	Phone:		Email:

HORSE INFORMATION	Name:		Breed:
	Gender:		Primary Use:
	Age:		Temperament (1-10):

Veterinarian:	HOOF ANGLES			HOOF LENGTHS		
		Left	Right		Left	Right
Trainer:	Front			Front		
	Back			Back		

Health Concerns:	Supplements:	Shoe Size:
		Shoe Type:
		Shoe Pads:
Therapeutic Treatments:	Special Requirements:	Dates Due:
Notes (Problems, Consultations, Changes, etc.):		Stable Name / Address:

CLIENT INFORMATION	Name:		
	Address:		
	Phone:		Email:

HORSE INFORMATION	Name:		Breed:
	Gender:		Primary Use:
	Age:		Temperament (1-10):

Veterinarian:	HOOF ANGLES			HOOF LENGTHS		
		Left	Right		Left	Right
Trainer:	Front			Front		
	Back			Back		

Health Concerns:	Supplements:	Shoe Size:
		Shoe Type:
		Shoe Pads:
Therapeutic Treatments:	Special Requirements:	Dates Due:
Notes (Problems, Consultations, Changes, etc.):		Stable Name / Address:

CLIENT INFORMATION	Name:	
	Address:	
	Phone:	Email:

HORSE INFORMATION	Name:	Breed:
	Gender:	Primary Use:
	Age:	Temperament (1-10):

Veterinarian:	HOOF ANGLES			HOOF LENGTHS		
		Left	Right		Left	Right
Trainer:	Front			Front		
	Back			Back		

Health Concerns:	Supplements:	Shoe Size:
		Shoe Type:
		Shoe Pads:
Therapeutic Treatments:	Special Requirements:	Dates Due:
Notes (Problems, Consultations, Changes, etc.):		Stable Name / Address:

CLIENT INFORMATION	Name:	
	Address:	
	Phone:	Email:

HORSE INFORMATION	Name:	Breed:
	Gender:	Primary Use:
	Age:	Temperament (1-10):

Veterinarian:	HOOF ANGLES			HOOF LENGTHS		
		Left	Right		Left	Right
Trainer:	Front			Front		
	Back			Back		

Health Concerns:	Supplements:	Shoe Size:
		Shoe Type:
		Shoe Pads:
Therapeutic Treatments:	Special Requirements:	Dates Due:
Notes (Problems, Consultations, Changes, etc.):		Stable Name / Address:

CLIENT INFORMATION	Name:	
	Address:	
	Phone:	Email:

HORSE INFORMATION	Name:	Breed:
	Gender:	Primary Use:
	Age:	Temperament (1-10):

Veterinarian:	HOOF ANGLES			HOOF LENGTHS		
		Left	Right		Left	Right
Trainer:	Front			Front		
	Back			Back		

Health Concerns:	Supplements:	Shoe Size:
		Shoe Type:
		Shoe Pads:
Therapeutic Treatments:	Special Requirements:	Dates Due:

Notes (Problems, Consultations, Changes, etc.):	Stable Name / Address:

CLIENT INFORMATION	Name:	
	Address:	
	Phone:	Email:

HORSE INFORMATION	Name:	Breed:
	Gender:	Primary Use:
	Age:	Temperament (1-10):

Veterinarian:	HOOF ANGLES			HOOF LENGTHS		
		Left	Right		Left	Right
Trainer:	Front			Front		
	Back			Back		

Health Concerns:	Supplements:	Shoe Size:
		Shoe Type:
		Shoe Pads:
Therapeutic Treatments:	Special Requirements:	Dates Due:

Notes (Problems, Consultations, Changes, etc.):	Stable Name / Address:

CLIENT INFORMATION	Name:		
	Address:		
	Phone:		Email:
HORSE INFORMATION	Name:		Breed:
	Gender:		Primary Use:
	Age:		Temperament (1-10):

Veterinarian:	HOOF ANGLES			HOOF LENGTHS		
		Left	Right		Left	Right
Trainer:	Front			Front		
	Back			Back		
Health Concerns:	Supplements:			Shoe Size:		
				Shoe Type:		
				Shoe Pads:		
Therapeutic Treatments:	Special Requirements:			Dates Due:		
Notes (Problems, Consultations, Changes, etc.):				Stable Name / Address:		

CLIENT INFORMATION	Name:		
	Address:		
	Phone:		Email:
HORSE INFORMATION	Name:		Breed:
	Gender:		Primary Use:
	Age:		Temperament (1-10):

Veterinarian:	HOOF ANGLES			HOOF LENGTHS		
		Left	Right		Left	Right
Trainer:	Front			Front		
	Back			Back		
Health Concerns:	Supplements:			Shoe Size:		
				Shoe Type:		
				Shoe Pads:		
Therapeutic Treatments:	Special Requirements:			Dates Due:		
Notes (Problems, Consultations, Changes, etc.):				Stable Name / Address:		

CLIENT INFORMATION	Name:	
	Address:	
	Phone:	Email:

HORSE INFORMATION	Name:	Breed:
	Gender:	Primary Use:
	Age:	Temperament (1-10):

Veterinarian:	HOOF ANGLES			HOOF LENGTHS		
		Left	Right		Left	Right
Trainer:	Front			Front		
	Back			Back		

Health Concerns:	Supplements:	Shoe Size:
		Shoe Type:
		Shoe Pads:
Therapeutic Treatments:	Special Requirements:	Dates Due:

Notes (Problems, Consultations, Changes, etc.):	Stable Name / Address:

CLIENT INFORMATION	Name:	
	Address:	
	Phone:	Email:

HORSE INFORMATION	Name:	Breed:
	Gender:	Primary Use:
	Age:	Temperament (1-10):

Veterinarian:	HOOF ANGLES			HOOF LENGTHS		
		Left	Right		Left	Right
Trainer:	Front			Front		
	Back			Back		

Health Concerns:	Supplements:	Shoe Size:
		Shoe Type:
		Shoe Pads:
Therapeutic Treatments:	Special Requirements:	Dates Due:

Notes (Problems, Consultations, Changes, etc.):	Stable Name / Address:

CLIENT INFORMATION	Name:		
	Address:		
	Phone:		Email:

HORSE INFORMATION	Name:		Breed:
	Gender:		Primary Use:
	Age:		Temperament (1-10):

Veterinarian:

	HOOF ANGLES			HOOF LENGTHS		
		Left	Right		Left	Right
Front				Front		
Back				Back		

Trainer:

Health Concerns:

Supplements:

Shoe Size:

Shoe Type:

Shoe Pads:

Therapeutic Treatments:

Special Requirements:

Dates Due:

Notes (Problems, Consultations, Changes, etc.):

Stable Name / Address:

CLIENT INFORMATION	Name:		
	Address:		
	Phone:		Email:

HORSE INFORMATION	Name:		Breed:
	Gender:		Primary Use:
	Age:		Temperament (1-10):

Veterinarian:

	HOOF ANGLES			HOOF LENGTHS		
		Left	Right		Left	Right
Front				Front		
Back				Back		

Trainer:

Health Concerns:

Supplements:

Shoe Size:

Shoe Type:

Shoe Pads:

Therapeutic Treatments:

Special Requirements:

Dates Due:

Notes (Problems, Consultations, Changes, etc.):

Stable Name / Address:

CLIENT INFORMATION	Name:	
	Address:	
	Phone:	Email:

HORSE INFORMATION	Name:	Breed:
	Gender:	Primary Use:
	Age:	Temperament (1-10):

Veterinarian:	HOOF ANGLES			HOOF LENGTHS		
		Left	Right		Left	Right
Trainer:	Front			Front		
	Back			Back		

Health Concerns:	Supplements:	Shoe Size:
		Shoe Type:
		Shoe Pads:
Therapeutic Treatments:	Special Requirements:	Dates Due:
Notes (Problems, Consultations, Changes, etc.):		Stable Name / Address:

CLIENT INFORMATION	Name:	
	Address:	
	Phone:	Email:

HORSE INFORMATION	Name:	Breed:
	Gender:	Primary Use:
	Age:	Temperament (1-10):

Veterinarian:	HOOF ANGLES			HOOF LENGTHS		
		Left	Right		Left	Right
Trainer:	Front			Front		
	Back			Back		

Health Concerns:	Supplements:	Shoe Size:
		Shoe Type:
		Shoe Pads:
Therapeutic Treatments:	Special Requirements:	Dates Due:
Notes (Problems, Consultations, Changes, etc.):		Stable Name / Address:

CLIENT INFORMATION	Name:					
	Address:					
	Phone:			Email:		
HORSE INFORMATION	Name:			Breed:		
	Gender:			Primary Use:		
	Age:			Temperament (1-10):		

Veterinarian:	HOOF ANGLES			HOOF LENGTHS		
		Left	Right		Left	Right
Trainer:	Front			Front		
	Back			Back		
Health Concerns:	Supplements:			Shoe Size:		
				Shoe Type:		
				Shoe Pads:		
Therapeutic Treatments:	Special Requirements:			Dates Due:		
Notes (Problems, Consultations, Changes, etc.):				Stable Name / Address:		

CLIENT INFORMATION	Name:					
	Address:					
	Phone:			Email:		
HORSE INFORMATION	Name:			Breed:		
	Gender:			Primary Use:		
	Age:			Temperament (1-10):		

Veterinarian:	HOOF ANGLES			HOOF LENGTHS		
		Left	Right		Left	Right
Trainer:	Front			Front		
	Back			Back		
Health Concerns:	Supplements:			Shoe Size:		
				Shoe Type:		
				Shoe Pads:		
Therapeutic Treatments:	Special Requirements:			Dates Due:		
Notes (Problems, Consultations, Changes, etc.):				Stable Name / Address:		

CLIENT INFORMATION	Name:						
	Address:						
	Phone:			Email:			
HORSE INFORMATION	Name:			Breed:			
	Gender:			Primary Use:			
	Age:			Temperament (1-10):			
Veterinarian:	HOOF ANGLES			HOOF LENGTHS			
		Left	Right			Left	Right
Trainer:	Front				Front		
	Back				Back		
Health Concerns:	Supplements:			Shoe Size:			
				Shoe Type:			
				Shoe Pads:			
Therapeutic Treatments:	Special Requirements:			Dates Due:			
Notes (Problems, Consultations, Changes, etc.):				Stable Name / Address:			

CLIENT INFORMATION	Name:						
	Address:						
	Phone:			Email:			
HORSE INFORMATION	Name:			Breed:			
	Gender:			Primary Use:			
	Age:			Temperament (1-10):			
Veterinarian:	HOOF ANGLES			HOOF LENGTHS			
		Left	Right			Left	Right
Trainer:	Front				Front		
	Back				Back		
Health Concerns:	Supplements:			Shoe Size:			
				Shoe Type:			
				Shoe Pads:			
Therapeutic Treatments:	Special Requirements:			Dates Due:			
Notes (Problems, Consultations, Changes, etc.):				Stable Name / Address:			

CLIENT INFORMATION	Name:						
	Address:						
	Phone:			Email:			
HORSE INFORMATION	Name:			Breed:			
	Gender:			Primary Use:			
	Age:			Temperament (1-10):			

Veterinarian:	HOOF ANGLES			HOOF LENGTHS		
		Left	Right		Left	Right
Trainer:	Front			Front		
	Back			Back		

Health Concerns:	Supplements:	Shoe Size:
		Shoe Type:
		Shoe Pads:
Therapeutic Treatments:	Special Requirements:	Dates Due:
Notes (Problems, Consultations, Changes, etc.):		Stable Name / Address:

CLIENT INFORMATION	Name:						
	Address:						
	Phone:			Email:			
HORSE INFORMATION	Name:			Breed:			
	Gender:			Primary Use:			
	Age:			Temperament (1-10):			

Veterinarian:	HOOF ANGLES			HOOF LENGTHS		
		Left	Right		Left	Right
Trainer:	Front			Front		
	Back			Back		

Health Concerns:	Supplements:	Shoe Size:
		Shoe Type:
		Shoe Pads:
Therapeutic Treatments:	Special Requirements:	Dates Due:
Notes (Problems, Consultations, Changes, etc.):		Stable Name / Address:

CLIENT INFORMATION	Name:					
	Address:					
	Phone:			Email:		
HORSE INFORMATION	Name:			Breed:		
	Gender:			Primary Use:		
	Age:			Temperament (1-10):		

Veterinarian:	HOOF ANGLES			HOOF LENGTHS		
		Left	Right		Left	Right
Trainer:	Front			Front		
	Back			Back		
Health Concerns:	Supplements:			Shoe Size:		
				Shoe Type:		
				Shoe Pads:		
Therapeutic Treatments:	Special Requirements:			Dates Due:		
Notes (Problems, Consultations, Changes, etc.):				Stable Name / Address:		

CLIENT INFORMATION	Name:					
	Address:					
	Phone:			Email:		
HORSE INFORMATION	Name:			Breed:		
	Gender:			Primary Use:		
	Age:			Temperament (1-10):		

Veterinarian:	HOOF ANGLES			HOOF LENGTHS		
		Left	Right		Left	Right
Trainer:	Front			Front		
	Back			Back		
Health Concerns:	Supplements:			Shoe Size:		
				Shoe Type:		
				Shoe Pads:		
Therapeutic Treatments:	Special Requirements:			Dates Due:		
Notes (Problems, Consultations, Changes, etc.):				Stable Name / Address:		

CLIENT INFORMATION	Name:						
	Address:						
	Phone:			Email:			
HORSE INFORMATION	Name:			Breed:			
	Gender:			Primary Use:			
	Age:			Temperament (1-10):			
Veterinarian:	HOOF ANGLES			HOOF LENGTHS			
		Left	Right		Left	Right	
Trainer:	Front			Front			
	Back			Back			
Health Concerns:	Supplements:			Shoe Size:			
				Shoe Type:			
				Shoe Pads:			
Therapeutic Treatments:	Special Requirements:			Dates Due:			
Notes (Problems, Consultations, Changes, etc.):				Stable Name / Address:			

CLIENT INFORMATION	Name:						
	Address:						
	Phone:			Email:			
HORSE INFORMATION	Name:			Breed:			
	Gender:			Primary Use:			
	Age:			Temperament (1-10):			
Veterinarian:	HOOF ANGLES			HOOF LENGTHS			
		Left	Right		Left	Right	
Trainer:	Front			Front			
	Back			Back			
Health Concerns:	Supplements:			Shoe Size:			
				Shoe Type:			
				Shoe Pads:			
Therapeutic Treatments:	Special Requirements:			Dates Due:			
Notes (Problems, Consultations, Changes, etc.):				Stable Name / Address:			

CLIENT INFORMATION	Name:						
	Address:						
	Phone:			Email:			
HORSE INFORMATION	Name:			Breed:			
	Gender:			Primary Use:			
	Age:			Temperament (1-10):			

Veterinarian:	HOOF ANGLES			HOOF LENGTHS		
		Left	Right		Left	Right
Trainer:	Front			Front		
	Back			Back		
Health Concerns:	Supplements:		Shoe Size:			
			Shoe Type:			
			Shoe Pads:			
Therapeutic Treatments:	Special Requirements:		Dates Due:			
Notes (Problems, Consultations, Changes, etc.):			Stable Name / Address:			

CLIENT INFORMATION	Name:						
	Address:						
	Phone:			Email:			
HORSE INFORMATION	Name:			Breed:			
	Gender:			Primary Use:			
	Age:			Temperament (1-10):			

Veterinarian:	HOOF ANGLES			HOOF LENGTHS		
		Left	Right		Left	Right
Trainer:	Front			Front		
	Back			Back		
Health Concerns:	Supplements:		Shoe Size:			
			Shoe Type:			
			Shoe Pads:			
Therapeutic Treatments:	Special Requirements:		Dates Due:			
Notes (Problems, Consultations, Changes, etc.):			Stable Name / Address:			

CLIENT INFORMATION	Name:	
	Address:	
	Phone:	Email:

HORSE INFORMATION	Name:	Breed:
	Gender:	Primary Use:
	Age:	Temperament (1-10):

		HOOF ANGLES			HOOF LENGTHS	
Veterinarian:		Left	Right		Left	Right
Trainer:	Front			Front		
	Back			Back		

Health Concerns:	Supplements:	Shoe Size:
		Shoe Type:
		Shoe Pads:
Therapeutic Treatments:	Special Requirements:	Dates Due:

Notes (Problems, Consultations, Changes, etc.):	Stable Name / Address:

CLIENT INFORMATION	Name:	
	Address:	
	Phone:	Email:

HORSE INFORMATION	Name:	Breed:
	Gender:	Primary Use:
	Age:	Temperament (1-10):

		HOOF ANGLES			HOOF LENGTHS	
Veterinarian:		Left	Right		Left	Right
Trainer:	Front			Front		
	Back			Back		

Health Concerns:	Supplements:	Shoe Size:
		Shoe Type:
		Shoe Pads:
Therapeutic Treatments:	Special Requirements:	Dates Due:

Notes (Problems, Consultations, Changes, etc.):	Stable Name / Address:

CLIENT INFORMATION	Name:		
	Address:		
	Phone:	Email:	

HORSE INFORMATION	Name:	Breed:
	Gender:	Primary Use:
	Age:	Temperament (1-10):

Veterinarian:	HOOF ANGLES			HOOF LENGTHS		
		Left	Right		Left	Right
Trainer:	Front			Front		
	Back			Back		

Health Concerns:	Supplements:	Shoe Size:
		Shoe Type:
		Shoe Pads:
Therapeutic Treatments:	Special Requirements:	Dates Due:

| Notes (Problems, Consultations, Changes, etc.): | Stable Name / Address: |

CLIENT INFORMATION	Name:		
	Address:		
	Phone:	Email:	

HORSE INFORMATION	Name:	Breed:
	Gender:	Primary Use:
	Age:	Temperament (1-10):

Veterinarian:	HOOF ANGLES			HOOF LENGTHS		
		Left	Right		Left	Right
Trainer:	Front			Front		
	Back			Back		

Health Concerns:	Supplements:	Shoe Size:
		Shoe Type:
		Shoe Pads:
Therapeutic Treatments:	Special Requirements:	Dates Due:

| Notes (Problems, Consultations, Changes, etc.): | Stable Name / Address: |

CLIENT INFORMATION	Name:		
	Address:		
	Phone:		Email:

HORSE INFORMATION	Name:		Breed:
	Gender:		Primary Use:
	Age:		Temperament (1-10):

Veterinarian:	HOOF ANGLES			HOOF LENGTHS		
		Left	Right		Left	Right
Trainer:	Front			Front		
	Back			Back		

Health Concerns:	Supplements:	Shoe Size:
		Shoe Type:
		Shoe Pads:
Therapeutic Treatments:	Special Requirements:	Dates Due:

| Notes (Problems, Consultations, Changes, etc.): | Stable Name / Address: |

CLIENT INFORMATION	Name:		
	Address:		
	Phone:		Email:

HORSE INFORMATION	Name:		Breed:
	Gender:		Primary Use:
	Age:		Temperament (1-10):

Veterinarian:	HOOF ANGLES			HOOF LENGTHS		
		Left	Right		Left	Right
Trainer:	Front			Front		
	Back			Back		

Health Concerns:	Supplements:	Shoe Size:
		Shoe Type:
		Shoe Pads:
Therapeutic Treatments:	Special Requirements:	Dates Due:

| Notes (Problems, Consultations, Changes, etc.): | Stable Name / Address: |

CLIENT INFORMATION	Name:						
	Address:						
	Phone:			Email:			
HORSE INFORMATION	Name:			Breed:			
	Gender:			Primary Use:			
	Age:			Temperament (1-10):			

Veterinarian:	HOOF ANGLES			HOOF LENGTHS		
		Left	Right		Left	Right
Trainer:	Front			Front		
	Back			Back		

Health Concerns:	Supplements:	Shoe Size:
		Shoe Type:
		Shoe Pads:
Therapeutic Treatments:	Special Requirements:	Dates Due:
Notes (Problems, Consultations, Changes, etc.):		Stable Name / Address:

CLIENT INFORMATION	Name:						
	Address:						
	Phone:			Email:			
HORSE INFORMATION	Name:			Breed:			
	Gender:			Primary Use:			
	Age:			Temperament (1-10):			

Veterinarian:	HOOF ANGLES			HOOF LENGTHS		
		Left	Right		Left	Right
Trainer:	Front			Front		
	Back			Back		

Health Concerns:	Supplements:	Shoe Size:
		Shoe Type:
		Shoe Pads:
Therapeutic Treatments:	Special Requirements:	Dates Due:
Notes (Problems, Consultations, Changes, etc.):		Stable Name / Address:

CLIENT INFORMATION	Name:						
	Address:						
	Phone:			Email:			
HORSE INFORMATION	Name:			Breed:			
	Gender:			Primary Use:			
	Age:			Temperament (1-10):			

Veterinarian:	HOOF ANGLES			HOOF LENGTHS		
		Left	Right		Left	Right
Trainer:	Front			Front		
	Back			Back		
Health Concerns:	Supplements:			Shoe Size:		
				Shoe Type:		
				Shoe Pads:		
Therapeutic Treatments:	Special Requirements:			Dates Due:		
Notes (Problems, Consultations, Changes, etc.):				Stable Name / Address:		

CLIENT INFORMATION	Name:						
	Address:						
	Phone:			Email:			
HORSE INFORMATION	Name:			Breed:			
	Gender:			Primary Use:			
	Age:			Temperament (1-10):			

Veterinarian:	HOOF ANGLES			HOOF LENGTHS		
		Left	Right		Left	Right
Trainer:	Front			Front		
	Back			Back		
Health Concerns:	Supplements:			Shoe Size:		
				Shoe Type:		
				Shoe Pads:		
Therapeutic Treatments:	Special Requirements:			Dates Due:		
Notes (Problems, Consultations, Changes, etc.):				Stable Name / Address:		

CLIENT INFORMATION	Name:		
	Address:		
	Phone:		Email:

HORSE INFORMATION	Name:		Breed:
	Gender:		Primary Use:
	Age:		Temperament (1-10):

Veterinarian:	HOOF ANGLES			HOOF LENGTHS		
		Left	Right		Left	Right
Trainer:	Front			Front		
	Back			Back		

Health Concerns:	Supplements:	Shoe Size:
		Shoe Type:
		Shoe Pads:
Therapeutic Treatments:	Special Requirements:	Dates Due:
Notes (Problems, Consultations, Changes, etc.):		Stable Name / Address:

CLIENT INFORMATION	Name:		
	Address:		
	Phone:		Email:

HORSE INFORMATION	Name:		Breed:
	Gender:		Primary Use:
	Age:		Temperament (1-10):

Veterinarian:	HOOF ANGLES			HOOF LENGTHS		
		Left	Right		Left	Right
Trainer:	Front			Front		
	Back			Back		

Health Concerns:	Supplements:	Shoe Size:
		Shoe Type:
		Shoe Pads:
Therapeutic Treatments:	Special Requirements:	Dates Due:
Notes (Problems, Consultations, Changes, etc.):		Stable Name / Address:

CLIENT INFORMATION	Name:					
	Address:					
	Phone:			Email:		
HORSE INFORMATION	Name:			Breed:		
	Gender:			Primary Use:		
	Age:			Temperament (1-10):		

Veterinarian:	HOOF ANGLES			HOOF LENGTHS		
		Left	Right		Left	Right
Trainer:	Front			Front		
	Back			Back		
Health Concerns:	Supplements:			Shoe Size:		
				Shoe Type:		
				Shoe Pads:		
Therapeutic Treatments:	Special Requirements:			Dates Due:		
Notes (Problems, Consultations, Changes, etc.):				Stable Name / Address:		

CLIENT INFORMATION	Name:					
	Address:					
	Phone:			Email:		
HORSE INFORMATION	Name:			Breed:		
	Gender:			Primary Use:		
	Age:			Temperament (1-10):		

Veterinarian:	HOOF ANGLES			HOOF LENGTHS		
		Left	Right		Left	Right
Trainer:	Front			Front		
	Back			Back		
Health Concerns:	Supplements:			Shoe Size:		
				Shoe Type:		
				Shoe Pads:		
Therapeutic Treatments:	Special Requirements:			Dates Due:		
Notes (Problems, Consultations, Changes, etc.):				Stable Name / Address:		

CLIENT INFORMATION	Name:						
	Address:						
	Phone:				Email:		
HORSE INFORMATION	Name:				Breed:		
	Gender:				Primary Use:		
	Age:				Temperament (1-10):		

Veterinarian:	HOOF ANGLES			HOOF LENGTHS		
		Left	Right		Left	Right
Trainer:	Front			Front		
	Back			Back		

Health Concerns:	Supplements:	Shoe Size:
		Shoe Type:
		Shoe Pads:
Therapeutic Treatments:	Special Requirements:	Dates Due:
Notes (Problems, Consultations, Changes, etc.):		Stable Name / Address:

CLIENT INFORMATION	Name:						
	Address:						
	Phone:				Email:		
HORSE INFORMATION	Name:				Breed:		
	Gender:				Primary Use:		
	Age:				Temperament (1-10):		

Veterinarian:	HOOF ANGLES			HOOF LENGTHS		
		Left	Right		Left	Right
Trainer:	Front			Front		
	Back			Back		

Health Concerns:	Supplements:	Shoe Size:
		Shoe Type:
		Shoe Pads:
Therapeutic Treatments:	Special Requirements:	Dates Due:
Notes (Problems, Consultations, Changes, etc.):		Stable Name / Address:

CLIENT INFORMATION	Name:	
	Address:	
	Phone:	Email:

HORSE INFORMATION	Name:	Breed:
	Gender:	Primary Use:
	Age:	Temperament (1-10):

Veterinarian:

	HOOF ANGLES			HOOF LENGTHS		
		Left	Right		Left	Right
Trainer:	Front			Front		
	Back			Back		

Health Concerns:	Supplements:	Shoe Size:
		Shoe Type:
		Shoe Pads:
Therapeutic Treatments:	Special Requirements:	Dates Due:
Notes (Problems, Consultations, Changes, etc.):		Stable Name / Address:

CLIENT INFORMATION	Name:	
	Address:	
	Phone:	Email:

HORSE INFORMATION	Name:	Breed:
	Gender:	Primary Use:
	Age:	Temperament (1-10):

Veterinarian:

	HOOF ANGLES			HOOF LENGTHS		
		Left	Right		Left	Right
Trainer:	Front			Front		
	Back			Back		

Health Concerns:	Supplements:	Shoe Size:
		Shoe Type:
		Shoe Pads:
Therapeutic Treatments:	Special Requirements:	Dates Due:
Notes (Problems, Consultations, Changes, etc.):		Stable Name / Address:

CLIENT INFORMATION	Name:		
	Address:		
	Phone:	Email:	

HORSE INFORMATION	Name:	Breed:	
	Gender:	Primary Use:	
	Age:	Temperament (1-10):	

Veterinarian:	HOOF ANGLES			HOOF LENGTHS		
		Left	Right		Left	Right
Trainer:	Front			Front		
	Back			Back		

Health Concerns:	Supplements:	Shoe Size:
		Shoe Type:
		Shoe Pads:
Therapeutic Treatments:	Special Requirements:	Dates Due:
Notes (Problems, Consultations, Changes, etc.):		Stable Name / Address:

CLIENT INFORMATION	Name:		
	Address:		
	Phone:	Email:	

HORSE INFORMATION	Name:	Breed:	
	Gender:	Primary Use:	
	Age:	Temperament (1-10):	

Veterinarian:	HOOF ANGLES			HOOF LENGTHS		
		Left	Right		Left	Right
Trainer:	Front			Front		
	Back			Back		

Health Concerns:	Supplements:	Shoe Size:
		Shoe Type:
		Shoe Pads:
Therapeutic Treatments:	Special Requirements:	Dates Due:
Notes (Problems, Consultations, Changes, etc.):		Stable Name / Address:

CLIENT INFORMATION	Name:			
	Address:			
	Phone:		Email:	

HORSE INFORMATION	Name:		Breed:	
	Gender:		Primary Use:	
	Age:		Temperament (1-10):	

Veterinarian:	HOOF ANGLES			HOOF LENGTHS		
		Left	Right		Left	Right
Trainer:	Front			Front		
	Back			Back		
Health Concerns:	Supplements:			Shoe Size:		
				Shoe Type:		
				Shoe Pads:		
Therapeutic Treatments:	Special Requirements:			Dates Due:		
Notes (Problems, Consultations, Changes, etc.):				Stable Name / Address:		

CLIENT INFORMATION	Name:			
	Address:			
	Phone:		Email:	

HORSE INFORMATION	Name:		Breed:	
	Gender:		Primary Use:	
	Age:		Temperament (1-10):	

Veterinarian:	HOOF ANGLES			HOOF LENGTHS		
		Left	Right		Left	Right
Trainer:	Front			Front		
	Back			Back		
Health Concerns:	Supplements:			Shoe Size:		
				Shoe Type:		
				Shoe Pads:		
Therapeutic Treatments:	Special Requirements:			Dates Due:		
Notes (Problems, Consultations, Changes, etc.):				Stable Name / Address:		

CLIENT INFORMATION	Name:						
	Address:						
	Phone:				Email:		
HORSE INFORMATION	Name:				Breed:		
	Gender:				Primary Use:		
	Age:				Temperament (1-10):		

Veterinarian:	HOOF ANGLES			HOOF LENGTHS		
		Left	Right		Left	Right
Trainer:	Front			Front		
	Back			Back		

Health Concerns:	Supplements:	Shoe Size:
		Shoe Type:
		Shoe Pads:
Therapeutic Treatments:	Special Requirements:	Dates Due:
Notes (Problems, Consultations, Changes, etc.):		Stable Name / Address:

CLIENT INFORMATION	Name:						
	Address:						
	Phone:				Email:		
HORSE INFORMATION	Name:				Breed:		
	Gender:				Primary Use:		
	Age:				Temperament (1-10):		

Veterinarian:	HOOF ANGLES			HOOF LENGTHS		
		Left	Right		Left	Right
Trainer:	Front			Front		
	Back			Back		

Health Concerns:	Supplements:	Shoe Size:
		Shoe Type:
		Shoe Pads:
Therapeutic Treatments:	Special Requirements:	Dates Due:
Notes (Problems, Consultations, Changes, etc.):		Stable Name / Address:

CLIENT INFORMATION	Name:						
	Address:						
	Phone:				Email:		

HORSE INFORMATION	Name:				Breed:		
	Gender:				Primary Use:		
	Age:				Temperament (1-10):		

Veterinarian:	HOOF ANGLES			HOOF LENGTHS			
		Left	Right			Left	Right
Trainer:	Front			Front			
	Back			Back			
Health Concerns:	Supplements:			Shoe Size:			
				Shoe Type:			
				Shoe Pads:			
Therapeutic Treatments:	Special Requirements:			Dates Due:			
Notes (Problems, Consultations, Changes, etc.):				Stable Name / Address:			

CLIENT INFORMATION	Name:						
	Address:						
	Phone:				Email:		

HORSE INFORMATION	Name:				Breed:		
	Gender:				Primary Use:		
	Age:				Temperament (1-10):		

Veterinarian:	HOOF ANGLES			HOOF LENGTHS			
		Left	Right			Left	Right
Trainer:	Front			Front			
	Back			Back			
Health Concerns:	Supplements:			Shoe Size:			
				Shoe Type:			
				Shoe Pads:			
Therapeutic Treatments:	Special Requirements:			Dates Due:			
Notes (Problems, Consultations, Changes, etc.):				Stable Name / Address:			

CLIENT INFORMATION	Name:			
	Address:			
	Phone:		Email:	

HORSE INFORMATION	Name:		Breed:	
	Gender:		Primary Use:	
	Age:		Temperament (1-10):	

Veterinarian:	HOOF ANGLES			HOOF LENGTHS		
		Left	Right		Left	Right
Trainer:	Front			Front		
	Back			Back		

Health Concerns:	Supplements:	Shoe Size:
		Shoe Type:
		Shoe Pads:
Therapeutic Treatments:	Special Requirements:	Dates Due:

Notes (Problems, Consultations, Changes, etc.):	Stable Name / Address:

CLIENT INFORMATION	Name:			
	Address:			
	Phone:		Email:	

HORSE INFORMATION	Name:		Breed:	
	Gender:		Primary Use:	
	Age:		Temperament (1-10):	

Veterinarian:	HOOF ANGLES			HOOF LENGTHS		
		Left	Right		Left	Right
Trainer:	Front			Front		
	Back			Back		

Health Concerns:	Supplements:	Shoe Size:
		Shoe Type:
		Shoe Pads:
Therapeutic Treatments:	Special Requirements:	Dates Due:

Notes (Problems, Consultations, Changes, etc.):	Stable Name / Address:

CLIENT INFORMATION	Name:		
	Address:		
	Phone:	Email:	
HORSE INFORMATION	Name:	Breed:	
	Gender:	Primary Use:	
	Age:	Temperament (1-10):	

Veterinarian:	HOOF ANGLES			HOOF LENGTHS		
		Left	Right		Left	Right
Trainer:	Front			Front		
	Back			Back		
Health Concerns:	Supplements:			Shoe Size:		
				Shoe Type:		
				Shoe Pads:		
Therapeutic Treatments:	Special Requirements:			Dates Due:		
Notes (Problems, Consultations, Changes, etc.):				Stable Name / Address:		

CLIENT INFORMATION	Name:		
	Address:		
	Phone:	Email:	
HORSE INFORMATION	Name:	Breed:	
	Gender:	Primary Use:	
	Age:	Temperament (1-10):	

Veterinarian:	HOOF ANGLES			HOOF LENGTHS		
		Left	Right		Left	Right
Trainer:	Front			Front		
	Back			Back		
Health Concerns:	Supplements:			Shoe Size:		
				Shoe Type:		
				Shoe Pads:		
Therapeutic Treatments:	Special Requirements:			Dates Due:		
Notes (Problems, Consultations, Changes, etc.):				Stable Name / Address:		

CLIENT INFORMATION	Name:		
	Address:		
	Phone:		Email:

HORSE INFORMATION	Name:		Breed:
	Gender:		Primary Use:
	Age:		Temperament (1-10):

Veterinarian:	HOOF ANGLES			HOOF LENGTHS		
		Left	Right		Left	Right
Trainer:	Front			Front		
	Back			Back		
Health Concerns:	Supplements:			Shoe Size:		
				Shoe Type:		
				Shoe Pads:		
Therapeutic Treatments:	Special Requirements:			Dates Due:		
Notes (Problems, Consultations, Changes, etc.):				Stable Name / Address:		

CLIENT INFORMATION	Name:		
	Address:		
	Phone:		Email:

HORSE INFORMATION	Name:		Breed:
	Gender:		Primary Use:
	Age:		Temperament (1-10):

Veterinarian:	HOOF ANGLES			HOOF LENGTHS		
		Left	Right		Left	Right
Trainer:	Front			Front		
	Back			Back		
Health Concerns:	Supplements:			Shoe Size:		
				Shoe Type:		
				Shoe Pads:		
Therapeutic Treatments:	Special Requirements:			Dates Due:		
Notes (Problems, Consultations, Changes, etc.):				Stable Name / Address:		

CLIENT INFORMATION	Name:		
	Address:		
	Phone:		Email:

HORSE INFORMATION	Name:		Breed:
	Gender:		Primary Use:
	Age:		Temperament (1-10):

Veterinarian:	HOOF ANGLES			HOOF LENGTHS		
		Left	Right		Left	Right
Trainer:	Front			Front		
	Back			Back		
Health Concerns:	Supplements:			Shoe Size:		
				Shoe Type:		
				Shoe Pads:		
Therapeutic Treatments:	Special Requirements:			Dates Due:		
Notes (Problems, Consultations, Changes, etc.):				Stable Name / Address:		

CLIENT INFORMATION	Name:		
	Address:		
	Phone:		Email:

HORSE INFORMATION	Name:		Breed:
	Gender:		Primary Use:
	Age:		Temperament (1-10):

Veterinarian:	HOOF ANGLES			HOOF LENGTHS		
		Left	Right		Left	Right
Trainer:	Front			Front		
	Back			Back		
Health Concerns:	Supplements:			Shoe Size:		
				Shoe Type:		
				Shoe Pads:		
Therapeutic Treatments:	Special Requirements:			Dates Due:		
Notes (Problems, Consultations, Changes, etc.):				Stable Name / Address:		

CLIENT INFORMATION	Name:		
	Address:		
	Phone:		Email:
HORSE INFORMATION	Name:		Breed:
	Gender:		Primary Use:
	Age:		Temperament (1-10):

Veterinarian:	HOOF ANGLES			HOOF LENGTHS		
		Left	Right		Left	Right
Trainer:	Front			Front		
	Back			Back		
Health Concerns:	Supplements:			Shoe Size:		
				Shoe Type:		
				Shoe Pads:		
Therapeutic Treatments:	Special Requirements:			Dates Due:		
Notes (Problems, Consultations, Changes, etc.):				Stable Name / Address:		

CLIENT INFORMATION	Name:		
	Address:		
	Phone:		Email:
HORSE INFORMATION	Name:		Breed:
	Gender:		Primary Use:
	Age:		Temperament (1-10):

Veterinarian:	HOOF ANGLES			HOOF LENGTHS		
		Left	Right		Left	Right
Trainer:	Front			Front		
	Back			Back		
Health Concerns:	Supplements:			Shoe Size:		
				Shoe Type:		
				Shoe Pads:		
Therapeutic Treatments:	Special Requirements:			Dates Due:		
Notes (Problems, Consultations, Changes, etc.):				Stable Name / Address:		

CLIENT INFORMATION	Name:		
	Address:		
	Phone:		Email:

HORSE INFORMATION	Name:		Breed:
	Gender:		Primary Use:
	Age:		Temperament (1-10):

Veterinarian:

HOOF ANGLES			HOOF LENGTHS		
	Left	Right		Left	Right
Front			Front		
Back			Back		

Trainer:

Health Concerns:

Supplements:	Shoe Size:
	Shoe Type:
	Shoe Pads:

Therapeutic Treatments:

Special Requirements:	Dates Due:

Notes (Problems, Consultations, Changes, etc.):	Stable Name / Address:

CLIENT INFORMATION	Name:		
	Address:		
	Phone:		Email:

HORSE INFORMATION	Name:		Breed:
	Gender:		Primary Use:
	Age:		Temperament (1-10):

Veterinarian:

HOOF ANGLES			HOOF LENGTHS		
	Left	Right		Left	Right
Front			Front		
Back			Back		

Trainer:

Health Concerns:

Supplements:	Shoe Size:
	Shoe Type:
	Shoe Pads:

Therapeutic Treatments:

Special Requirements:	Dates Due:

Notes (Problems, Consultations, Changes, etc.):	Stable Name / Address:

CLIENT INFORMATION	Name:						
	Address:						
	Phone:			Email:			
HORSE INFORMATION	Name:			Breed:			
	Gender:			Primary Use:			
	Age:			Temperament (1-10):			
Veterinarian:	HOOF ANGLES			HOOF LENGTHS			
		Left	Right		Left	Right	
Trainer:	Front			Front			
	Back			Back			
Health Concerns:	Supplements:			Shoe Size:			
				Shoe Type:			
				Shoe Pads:			
Therapeutic Treatments:	Special Requirements:			Dates Due:			
Notes (Problems, Consultations, Changes, etc.):				Stable Name / Address:			

CLIENT INFORMATION	Name:						
	Address:						
	Phone:			Email:			
HORSE INFORMATION	Name:			Breed:			
	Gender:			Primary Use:			
	Age:			Temperament (1-10):			
Veterinarian:	HOOF ANGLES			HOOF LENGTHS			
		Left	Right		Left	Right	
Trainer:	Front			Front			
	Back			Back			
Health Concerns:	Supplements:			Shoe Size:			
				Shoe Type:			
				Shoe Pads:			
Therapeutic Treatments:	Special Requirements:			Dates Due:			
Notes (Problems, Consultations, Changes, etc.):				Stable Name / Address:			

CLIENT INFORMATION	Name:						
	Address:						
	Phone:				Email:		
HORSE INFORMATION	Name:				Breed:		
	Gender:				Primary Use:		
	Age:				Temperament (1-10):		

Veterinarian:	HOOF ANGLES			HOOF LENGTHS		
		Left	Right		Left	Right
Trainer:	Front			Front		
	Back			Back		

Health Concerns:	Supplements:	Shoe Size:
		Shoe Type:
		Shoe Pads:
Therapeutic Treatments:	Special Requirements:	Dates Due:
Notes (Problems, Consultations, Changes, etc.):		Stable Name / Address:

CLIENT INFORMATION	Name:						
	Address:						
	Phone:				Email:		
HORSE INFORMATION	Name:				Breed:		
	Gender:				Primary Use:		
	Age:				Temperament (1-10):		

Veterinarian:	HOOF ANGLES			HOOF LENGTHS		
		Left	Right		Left	Right
Trainer:	Front			Front		
	Back			Back		

Health Concerns:	Supplements:	Shoe Size:
		Shoe Type:
		Shoe Pads:
Therapeutic Treatments:	Special Requirements:	Dates Due:
Notes (Problems, Consultations, Changes, etc.):		Stable Name / Address:

CLIENT INFORMATION	Name:		
	Address:		
	Phone:		Email:

HORSE INFORMATION	Name:		Breed:
	Gender:		Primary Use:
	Age:		Temperament (1-10):

Veterinarian:	HOOF ANGLES			HOOF LENGTHS		
		Left	Right		Left	Right
Trainer:	Front			Front		
	Back			Back		

Health Concerns:	Supplements:	Shoe Size:
		Shoe Type:
		Shoe Pads:
Therapeutic Treatments:	Special Requirements:	Dates Due:
Notes (Problems, Consultations, Changes, etc.):		Stable Name / Address:

CLIENT INFORMATION	Name:		
	Address:		
	Phone:		Email:

HORSE INFORMATION	Name:		Breed:
	Gender:		Primary Use:
	Age:		Temperament (1-10):

Veterinarian:	HOOF ANGLES			HOOF LENGTHS		
		Left	Right		Left	Right
Trainer:	Front			Front		
	Back			Back		

Health Concerns:	Supplements:	Shoe Size:
		Shoe Type:
		Shoe Pads:
Therapeutic Treatments:	Special Requirements:	Dates Due:
Notes (Problems, Consultations, Changes, etc.):		Stable Name / Address:

CLIENT INFORMATION	Name:				
	Address:				
	Phone:		Email:		
HORSE INFORMATION	Name:		Breed:		
	Gender:		Primary Use:		
	Age:		Temperament (1-10):		

Veterinarian:	HOOF ANGLES			HOOF LENGTHS		
		Left	Right		Left	Right
Trainer:	Front			Front		
	Back			Back		

Health Concerns:	Supplements:	Shoe Size:
		Shoe Type:
		Shoe Pads:
Therapeutic Treatments:	Special Requirements:	Dates Due:
Notes (Problems, Consultations, Changes, etc.):		Stable Name / Address:

CLIENT INFORMATION	Name:				
	Address:				
	Phone:		Email:		
HORSE INFORMATION	Name:		Breed:		
	Gender:		Primary Use:		
	Age:		Temperament (1-10):		

Veterinarian:	HOOF ANGLES			HOOF LENGTHS		
		Left	Right		Left	Right
Trainer:	Front			Front		
	Back			Back		

Health Concerns:	Supplements:	Shoe Size:
		Shoe Type:
		Shoe Pads:
Therapeutic Treatments:	Special Requirements:	Dates Due:
Notes (Problems, Consultations, Changes, etc.):		Stable Name / Address:

CLIENT INFORMATION	Name:					
	Address:					
	Phone:			Email:		
HORSE INFORMATION	Name:			Breed:		
	Gender:			Primary Use:		
	Age:			Temperament (1-10):		

Veterinarian:	HOOF ANGLES			HOOF LENGTHS		
		Left	Right		Left	Right
Trainer:	Front			Front		
	Back			Back		
Health Concerns:	Supplements:			Shoe Size:		
				Shoe Type:		
				Shoe Pads:		
Therapeutic Treatments:	Special Requirements:			Dates Due:		
Notes (Problems, Consultations, Changes, etc.):				Stable Name / Address:		

CLIENT INFORMATION	Name:					
	Address:					
	Phone:			Email:		
HORSE INFORMATION	Name:			Breed:		
	Gender:			Primary Use:		
	Age:			Temperament (1-10):		

Veterinarian:	HOOF ANGLES			HOOF LENGTHS		
		Left	Right		Left	Right
Trainer:	Front			Front		
	Back			Back		
Health Concerns:	Supplements:			Shoe Size:		
				Shoe Type:		
				Shoe Pads:		
Therapeutic Treatments:	Special Requirements:			Dates Due:		
Notes (Problems, Consultations, Changes, etc.):				Stable Name / Address:		

CLIENT INFORMATION	Name:					
	Address:					
	Phone:			Email:		
HORSE INFORMATION	Name:			Breed:		
	Gender:			Primary Use:		
	Age:			Temperament (1-10):		

Veterinarian:	HOOF ANGLES			HOOF LENGTHS		
		Left	Right		Left	Right
Trainer:	Front			Front		
	Back			Back		
Health Concerns:	Supplements:			Shoe Size:		
				Shoe Type:		
				Shoe Pads:		
Therapeutic Treatments:	Special Requirements:			Dates Due:		
Notes (Problems, Consultations, Changes, etc.):				Stable Name / Address:		

CLIENT INFORMATION	Name:					
	Address:					
	Phone:			Email:		
HORSE INFORMATION	Name:			Breed:		
	Gender:			Primary Use:		
	Age:			Temperament (1-10):		

Veterinarian:	HOOF ANGLES			HOOF LENGTHS		
		Left	Right		Left	Right
Trainer:	Front			Front		
	Back			Back		
Health Concerns:	Supplements:			Shoe Size:		
				Shoe Type:		
				Shoe Pads:		
Therapeutic Treatments:	Special Requirements:			Dates Due:		
Notes (Problems, Consultations, Changes, etc.):				Stable Name / Address:		

CLIENT INFORMATION	Name:						
	Address:						
	Phone:			Email:			
HORSE INFORMATION	Name:			Breed:			
	Gender:			Primary Use:			
	Age:			Temperament (1-10):			

Veterinarian:	HOOF ANGLES			HOOF LENGTHS		
		Left	Right		Left	Right
Trainer:	Front			Front		
	Back			Back		
Health Concerns:	Supplements:			Shoe Size:		
				Shoe Type:		
				Shoe Pads:		
Therapeutic Treatments:	Special Requirements:			Dates Due:		
Notes (Problems, Consultations, Changes, etc.):				Stable Name / Address:		

CLIENT INFORMATION	Name:						
	Address:						
	Phone:			Email:			
HORSE INFORMATION	Name:			Breed:			
	Gender:			Primary Use:			
	Age:			Temperament (1-10):			

Veterinarian:	HOOF ANGLES			HOOF LENGTHS		
		Left	Right		Left	Right
Trainer:	Front			Front		
	Back			Back		
Health Concerns:	Supplements:			Shoe Size:		
				Shoe Type:		
				Shoe Pads:		
Therapeutic Treatments:	Special Requirements:			Dates Due:		
Notes (Problems, Consultations, Changes, etc.):				Stable Name / Address:		

CLIENT INFORMATION	Name:		
	Address:		
	Phone:	Email:	
HORSE INFORMATION	Name:	Breed:	
	Gender:	Primary Use:	
	Age:	Temperament (1-10):	

Veterinarian:	HOOF ANGLES			HOOF LENGTHS		
		Left	Right		Left	Right
Trainer:	Front			Front		
	Back			Back		
Health Concerns:	Supplements:			Shoe Size:		
				Shoe Type:		
				Shoe Pads:		
Therapeutic Treatments:	Special Requirements:			Dates Due:		
Notes (Problems, Consultations, Changes, etc.):				Stable Name / Address:		

CLIENT INFORMATION	Name:		
	Address:		
	Phone:	Email:	
HORSE INFORMATION	Name:	Breed:	
	Gender:	Primary Use:	
	Age:	Temperament (1-10):	

Veterinarian:	HOOF ANGLES			HOOF LENGTHS		
		Left	Right		Left	Right
Trainer:	Front			Front		
	Back			Back		
Health Concerns:	Supplements:			Shoe Size:		
				Shoe Type:		
				Shoe Pads:		
Therapeutic Treatments:	Special Requirements:			Dates Due:		
Notes (Problems, Consultations, Changes, etc.):				Stable Name / Address:		

CLIENT INFORMATION	Name:	
	Address:	
	Phone:	Email:

HORSE INFORMATION	Name:	Breed:
	Gender:	Primary Use:
	Age:	Temperament (1-10):

Veterinarian:	HOOF ANGLES			HOOF LENGTHS		
		Left	Right		Left	Right
Trainer:	Front			Front		
	Back			Back		

Health Concerns:	Supplements:		Shoe Size:
			Shoe Type:
			Shoe Pads:
Therapeutic Treatments:	Special Requirements:		Dates Due:

| Notes (Problems, Consultations, Changes, etc.): | Stable Name / Address: |

CLIENT INFORMATION	Name:	
	Address:	
	Phone:	Email:

HORSE INFORMATION	Name:	Breed:
	Gender:	Primary Use:
	Age:	Temperament (1-10):

Veterinarian:	HOOF ANGLES			HOOF LENGTHS		
		Left	Right		Left	Right
Trainer:	Front			Front		
	Back			Back		

Health Concerns:	Supplements:		Shoe Size:
			Shoe Type:
			Shoe Pads:
Therapeutic Treatments:	Special Requirements:		Dates Due:

| Notes (Problems, Consultations, Changes, etc.): | Stable Name / Address: |

CLIENT INFORMATION	Name:					
	Address:					
	Phone:			Email:		
HORSE INFORMATION	Name:			Breed:		
	Gender:			Primary Use:		
	Age:			Temperament (1-10):		

Veterinarian:	HOOF ANGLES			HOOF LENGTHS		
		Left	Right		Left	Right
Trainer:	Front			Front		
	Back			Back		
Health Concerns:	Supplements:			Shoe Size:		
				Shoe Type:		
				Shoe Pads:		
Therapeutic Treatments:	Special Requirements:			Dates Due:		
Notes (Problems, Consultations, Changes, etc.):				Stable Name / Address:		

CLIENT INFORMATION	Name:					
	Address:					
	Phone:			Email:		
HORSE INFORMATION	Name:			Breed:		
	Gender:			Primary Use:		
	Age:			Temperament (1-10):		

Veterinarian:	HOOF ANGLES			HOOF LENGTHS		
		Left	Right		Left	Right
Trainer:	Front			Front		
	Back			Back		
Health Concerns:	Supplements:			Shoe Size:		
				Shoe Type:		
				Shoe Pads:		
Therapeutic Treatments:	Special Requirements:			Dates Due:		
Notes (Problems, Consultations, Changes, etc.):				Stable Name / Address:		

CLIENT INFORMATION	Name:						
	Address:						
	Phone:			Email:			
HORSE INFORMATION	Name:			Breed:			
	Gender:			Primary Use:			
	Age:			Temperament (1-10):			

Veterinarian:	HOOF ANGLES			HOOF LENGTHS			
		Left	Right			Left	Right
Trainer:	Front				Front		
	Back				Back		
Health Concerns:	Supplements:			Shoe Size:			
				Shoe Type:			
				Shoe Pads:			
Therapeutic Treatments:	Special Requirements:			Dates Due:			
Notes (Problems, Consultations, Changes, etc.):				Stable Name / Address:			

CLIENT INFORMATION	Name:						
	Address:						
	Phone:			Email:			
HORSE INFORMATION	Name:			Breed:			
	Gender:			Primary Use:			
	Age:			Temperament (1-10):			

Veterinarian:	HOOF ANGLES			HOOF LENGTHS			
		Left	Right			Left	Right
Trainer:	Front				Front		
	Back				Back		
Health Concerns:	Supplements:			Shoe Size:			
				Shoe Type:			
				Shoe Pads:			
Therapeutic Treatments:	Special Requirements:			Dates Due:			
Notes (Problems, Consultations, Changes, etc.):				Stable Name / Address:			

CLIENT INFORMATION	Name:						
	Address:						
	Phone:			Email:			
HORSE INFORMATION	Name:			Breed:			
	Gender:			Primary Use:			
	Age:			Temperament (1-10):			
Veterinarian:	HOOF ANGLES			HOOF LENGTHS			
		Left	Right			Left	Right
Trainer:	Front				Front		
	Back				Back		
Health Concerns:	Supplements:			Shoe Size:			
				Shoe Type:			
				Shoe Pads:			
Therapeutic Treatments:	Special Requirements:			Dates Due:			
Notes (Problems, Consultations, Changes, etc.):				Stable Name / Address:			

CLIENT INFORMATION	Name:						
	Address:						
	Phone:			Email:			
HORSE INFORMATION	Name:			Breed:			
	Gender:			Primary Use:			
	Age:			Temperament (1-10):			
Veterinarian:	HOOF ANGLES			HOOF LENGTHS			
		Left	Right			Left	Right
Trainer:	Front				Front		
	Back				Back		
Health Concerns:	Supplements:			Shoe Size:			
				Shoe Type:			
				Shoe Pads:			
Therapeutic Treatments:	Special Requirements:			Dates Due:			
Notes (Problems, Consultations, Changes, etc.):				Stable Name / Address:			

CLIENT INFORMATION	Name:						
	Address:						
	Phone:			Email:			
HORSE INFORMATION	Name:			Breed:			
	Gender:			Primary Use:			
	Age:			Temperament (1-10):			
Veterinarian:	HOOF ANGLES			HOOF LENGTHS			
		Left	Right			Left	Right
Trainer:	Front				Front		
	Back				Back		
Health Concerns:	Supplements:			Shoe Size:			
				Shoe Type:			
				Shoe Pads:			
Therapeutic Treatments:	Special Requirements:			Dates Due:			
Notes (Problems, Consultations, Changes, etc.):				Stable Name / Address:			

CLIENT INFORMATION	Name:						
	Address:						
	Phone:			Email:			
HORSE INFORMATION	Name:			Breed:			
	Gender:			Primary Use:			
	Age:			Temperament (1-10):			
Veterinarian:	HOOF ANGLES			HOOF LENGTHS			
		Left	Right			Left	Right
Trainer:	Front				Front		
	Back				Back		
Health Concerns:	Supplements:			Shoe Size:			
				Shoe Type:			
				Shoe Pads:			
Therapeutic Treatments:	Special Requirements:			Dates Due:			
Notes (Problems, Consultations, Changes, etc.):				Stable Name / Address:			

CLIENT INFORMATION	Name:		
	Address:		
	Phone:		Email:

HORSE INFORMATION	Name:		Breed:
	Gender:		Primary Use:
	Age:		Temperament (1-10):

Veterinarian:

HOOF ANGLES			HOOF LENGTHS		
	Left	Right		Left	Right
Front			Front		
Back			Back		

Trainer:

Health Concerns:

Supplements:	Shoe Size:
	Shoe Type:
	Shoe Pads:

Therapeutic Treatments:

Special Requirements:	Dates Due:

Notes (Problems, Consultations, Changes, etc.):	Stable Name / Address:

CLIENT INFORMATION	Name:		
	Address:		
	Phone:		Email:

HORSE INFORMATION	Name:		Breed:
	Gender:		Primary Use:
	Age:		Temperament (1-10):

Veterinarian:

HOOF ANGLES			HOOF LENGTHS		
	Left	Right		Left	Right
Front			Front		
Back			Back		

Trainer:

Health Concerns:

Supplements:	Shoe Size:
	Shoe Type:
	Shoe Pads:

Therapeutic Treatments:

Special Requirements:	Dates Due:

Notes (Problems, Consultations, Changes, etc.):	Stable Name / Address:

CLIENT INFORMATION	Name:		
	Address:		
	Phone:		Email:

HORSE INFORMATION	Name:		Breed:
	Gender:		Primary Use:
	Age:		Temperament (1-10):

Veterinarian:	HOOF ANGLES			HOOF LENGTHS		
		Left	Right		Left	Right
Trainer:	Front			Front		
	Back			Back		
Health Concerns:	Supplements:			Shoe Size:		
				Shoe Type:		
				Shoe Pads:		
Therapeutic Treatments:	Special Requirements:			Dates Due:		
Notes (Problems, Consultations, Changes, etc.):				Stable Name / Address:		

CLIENT INFORMATION	Name:		
	Address:		
	Phone:		Email:

HORSE INFORMATION	Name:		Breed:
	Gender:		Primary Use:
	Age:		Temperament (1-10):

Veterinarian:	HOOF ANGLES			HOOF LENGTHS		
		Left	Right		Left	Right
Trainer:	Front			Front		
	Back			Back		
Health Concerns:	Supplements:			Shoe Size:		
				Shoe Type:		
				Shoe Pads:		
Therapeutic Treatments:	Special Requirements:			Dates Due:		
Notes (Problems, Consultations, Changes, etc.):				Stable Name / Address:		

CLIENT INFORMATION	Name:	
	Address:	
	Phone:	Email:

HORSE INFORMATION	Name:	Breed:
	Gender:	Primary Use:
	Age:	Temperament (1-10):

Veterinarian:	HOOF ANGLES			HOOF LENGTHS		
		Left	Right		Left	Right
Trainer:	Front			Front		
	Back			Back		
Health Concerns:	Supplements:			Shoe Size:		
				Shoe Type:		
				Shoe Pads:		
Therapeutic Treatments:	Special Requirements:			Dates Due:		
Notes (Problems, Consultations, Changes, etc.):				Stable Name / Address:		

CLIENT INFORMATION	Name:	
	Address:	
	Phone:	Email:

HORSE INFORMATION	Name:	Breed:
	Gender:	Primary Use:
	Age:	Temperament (1-10):

Veterinarian:	HOOF ANGLES			HOOF LENGTHS		
		Left	Right		Left	Right
Trainer:	Front			Front		
	Back			Back		
Health Concerns:	Supplements:			Shoe Size:		
				Shoe Type:		
				Shoe Pads:		
Therapeutic Treatments:	Special Requirements:			Dates Due:		
Notes (Problems, Consultations, Changes, etc.):				Stable Name / Address:		

CLIENT INFORMATION	Name:		
	Address:		
	Phone:		Email:

HORSE INFORMATION	Name:		Breed:
	Gender:		Primary Use:
	Age:		Temperament (1-10):

Veterinarian:	HOOF ANGLES			HOOF LENGTHS		
		Left	Right		Left	Right
Trainer:	Front			Front		
	Back			Back		

Health Concerns:	Supplements:	Shoe Size:
		Shoe Type:
		Shoe Pads:
Therapeutic Treatments:	Special Requirements:	Dates Due:
Notes (Problems, Consultations, Changes, etc.):		Stable Name / Address:

CLIENT INFORMATION	Name:		
	Address:		
	Phone:		Email:

HORSE INFORMATION	Name:		Breed:
	Gender:		Primary Use:
	Age:		Temperament (1-10):

Veterinarian:	HOOF ANGLES			HOOF LENGTHS		
		Left	Right		Left	Right
Trainer:	Front			Front		
	Back			Back		

Health Concerns:	Supplements:	Shoe Size:
		Shoe Type:
		Shoe Pads:
Therapeutic Treatments:	Special Requirements:	Dates Due:
Notes (Problems, Consultations, Changes, etc.):		Stable Name / Address:

CLIENT INFORMATION	Name:		
	Address:		
	Phone:		Email:
HORSE INFORMATION	Name:		Breed:
	Gender:		Primary Use:
	Age:		Temperament (1-10):

Veterinarian:	HOOF ANGLES			HOOF LENGTHS		
		Left	Right		Left	Right
Trainer:	Front			Front		
	Back			Back		
Health Concerns:	Supplements:			Shoe Size:		
				Shoe Type:		
				Shoe Pads:		
Therapeutic Treatments:	Special Requirements:			Dates Due:		
Notes (Problems, Consultations, Changes, etc.):				Stable Name / Address:		

CLIENT INFORMATION	Name:		
	Address:		
	Phone:		Email:
HORSE INFORMATION	Name:		Breed:
	Gender:		Primary Use:
	Age:		Temperament (1-10):

Veterinarian:	HOOF ANGLES			HOOF LENGTHS		
		Left	Right		Left	Right
Trainer:	Front			Front		
	Back			Back		
Health Concerns:	Supplements:			Shoe Size:		
				Shoe Type:		
				Shoe Pads:		
Therapeutic Treatments:	Special Requirements:			Dates Due:		
Notes (Problems, Consultations, Changes, etc.):				Stable Name / Address:		

CLIENT INFORMATION	Name:					
	Address:					
	Phone:			Email:		
HORSE INFORMATION	Name:			Breed:		
	Gender:			Primary Use:		
	Age:			Temperament (1-10):		

Veterinarian:	HOOF ANGLES			HOOF LENGTHS		
		Left	Right		Left	Right
Trainer:	Front			Front		
	Back			Back		
Health Concerns:	Supplements:			Shoe Size:		
				Shoe Type:		
				Shoe Pads:		
Therapeutic Treatments:	Special Requirements:			Dates Due:		
Notes (Problems, Consultations, Changes, etc.):				Stable Name / Address:		

CLIENT INFORMATION	Name:					
	Address:					
	Phone:			Email:		
HORSE INFORMATION	Name:			Breed:		
	Gender:			Primary Use:		
	Age:			Temperament (1-10):		

Veterinarian:	HOOF ANGLES			HOOF LENGTHS		
		Left	Right		Left	Right
Trainer:	Front			Front		
	Back			Back		
Health Concerns:	Supplements:			Shoe Size:		
				Shoe Type:		
				Shoe Pads:		
Therapeutic Treatments:	Special Requirements:			Dates Due:		
Notes (Problems, Consultations, Changes, etc.):				Stable Name / Address:		

CLIENT INFORMATION	Name:		
	Address:		
	Phone:		Email:

HORSE INFORMATION	Name:		Breed:
	Gender:		Primary Use:
	Age:		Temperament (1-10):

Veterinarian:	HOOF ANGLES			HOOF LENGTHS		
		Left	Right		Left	Right
Trainer:	Front			Front		
	Back			Back		

Health Concerns:	Supplements:	Shoe Size:
		Shoe Type:
		Shoe Pads:
Therapeutic Treatments:	Special Requirements:	Dates Due:
Notes (Problems, Consultations, Changes, etc.):		Stable Name / Address:

CLIENT INFORMATION	Name:		
	Address:		
	Phone:		Email:

HORSE INFORMATION	Name:		Breed:
	Gender:		Primary Use:
	Age:		Temperament (1-10):

Veterinarian:	HOOF ANGLES			HOOF LENGTHS		
		Left	Right		Left	Right
Trainer:	Front			Front		
	Back			Back		

Health Concerns:	Supplements:	Shoe Size:
		Shoe Type:
		Shoe Pads:
Therapeutic Treatments:	Special Requirements:	Dates Due:
Notes (Problems, Consultations, Changes, etc.):		Stable Name / Address:

CLIENT INFORMATION	Name:						
	Address:						
	Phone:			Email:			
HORSE INFORMATION	Name:			Breed:			
	Gender:			Primary Use:			
	Age:			Temperament (1-10):			

Veterinarian:	HOOF ANGLES			HOOF LENGTHS		
		Left	Right		Left	Right
Trainer:	Front			Front		
	Back			Back		

Health Concerns:	Supplements:	Shoe Size:
		Shoe Type:
		Shoe Pads:
Therapeutic Treatments:	Special Requirements:	Dates Due:

Notes (Problems, Consultations, Changes, etc.):	Stable Name / Address:

CLIENT INFORMATION	Name:						
	Address:						
	Phone:			Email:			
HORSE INFORMATION	Name:			Breed:			
	Gender:			Primary Use:			
	Age:			Temperament (1-10):			

Veterinarian:	HOOF ANGLES			HOOF LENGTHS		
		Left	Right		Left	Right
Trainer:	Front			Front		
	Back			Back		

Health Concerns:	Supplements:	Shoe Size:
		Shoe Type:
		Shoe Pads:
Therapeutic Treatments:	Special Requirements:	Dates Due:

Notes (Problems, Consultations, Changes, etc.):	Stable Name / Address:

CLIENT INFORMATION	Name:						
	Address:						
	Phone:				Email:		
HORSE INFORMATION	Name:				Breed:		
	Gender:				Primary Use:		
	Age:				Temperament (1-10):		

Veterinarian:	HOOF ANGLES			HOOF LENGTHS		
		Left	Right		Left	Right
Trainer:	Front			Front		
	Back			Back		

Health Concerns:	Supplements:	Shoe Size:
		Shoe Type:
		Shoe Pads:
Therapeutic Treatments:	Special Requirements:	Dates Due:
Notes (Problems, Consultations, Changes, etc.):		Stable Name / Address:

CLIENT INFORMATION	Name:						
	Address:						
	Phone:				Email:		
HORSE INFORMATION	Name:				Breed:		
	Gender:				Primary Use:		
	Age:				Temperament (1-10):		

Veterinarian:	HOOF ANGLES			HOOF LENGTHS		
		Left	Right		Left	Right
Trainer:	Front			Front		
	Back			Back		

Health Concerns:	Supplements:	Shoe Size:
		Shoe Type:
		Shoe Pads:
Therapeutic Treatments:	Special Requirements:	Dates Due:
Notes (Problems, Consultations, Changes, etc.):		Stable Name / Address:

CLIENT INFORMATION	Name:		
	Address:		
	Phone:	Email:	

HORSE INFORMATION	Name:	Breed:	
	Gender:	Primary Use:	
	Age:	Temperament (1-10):	

Veterinarian:	HOOF ANGLES			HOOF LENGTHS		
		Left	Right		Left	Right
Trainer:	Front			Front		
	Back			Back		
Health Concerns:	Supplements:		Shoe Size:		
			Shoe Type:		
			Shoe Pads:		
Therapeutic Treatments:	Special Requirements:		Dates Due:		
Notes (Problems, Consultations, Changes, etc.):			Stable Name / Address:		

CLIENT INFORMATION	Name:		
	Address:		
	Phone:	Email:	

HORSE INFORMATION	Name:	Breed:	
	Gender:	Primary Use:	
	Age:	Temperament (1-10):	

Veterinarian:	HOOF ANGLES			HOOF LENGTHS		
		Left	Right		Left	Right
Trainer:	Front			Front		
	Back			Back		
Health Concerns:	Supplements:		Shoe Size:		
			Shoe Type:		
			Shoe Pads:		
Therapeutic Treatments:	Special Requirements:		Dates Due:		
Notes (Problems, Consultations, Changes, etc.):			Stable Name / Address:		

CLIENT INFORMATION	Name:	
	Address:	
	Phone:	Email:
HORSE INFORMATION	Name:	Breed:
	Gender:	Primary Use:
	Age:	Temperament (1-10):

Veterinarian:	HOOF ANGLES			HOOF LENGTHS		
		Left	Right		Left	Right
Trainer:	Front			Front		
	Back			Back		
Health Concerns:	Supplements:			Shoe Size:		
				Shoe Type:		
				Shoe Pads:		
Therapeutic Treatments:	Special Requirements:			Dates Due:		
Notes (Problems, Consultations, Changes, etc.):				Stable Name / Address:		

CLIENT INFORMATION	Name:	
	Address:	
	Phone:	Email:
HORSE INFORMATION	Name:	Breed:
	Gender:	Primary Use:
	Age:	Temperament (1-10):

Veterinarian:	HOOF ANGLES			HOOF LENGTHS		
		Left	Right		Left	Right
Trainer:	Front			Front		
	Back			Back		
Health Concerns:	Supplements:			Shoe Size:		
				Shoe Type:		
				Shoe Pads:		
Therapeutic Treatments:	Special Requirements:			Dates Due:		
Notes (Problems, Consultations, Changes, etc.):				Stable Name / Address:		

CLIENT INFORMATION	Name:						
	Address:						
	Phone:				Email:		

HORSE INFORMATION	Name:				Breed:		
	Gender:				Primary Use:		
	Age:				Temperament (1-10):		

Veterinarian:	HOOF ANGLES			HOOF LENGTHS		
		Left	Right		Left	Right
Trainer:	Front			Front		
	Back			Back		

Health Concerns:	Supplements:	Shoe Size:
		Shoe Type:
		Shoe Pads:
Therapeutic Treatments:	Special Requirements:	Dates Due:
Notes (Problems, Consultations, Changes, etc.):		Stable Name / Address:

CLIENT INFORMATION	Name:						
	Address:						
	Phone:				Email:		

HORSE INFORMATION	Name:				Breed:		
	Gender:				Primary Use:		
	Age:				Temperament (1-10):		

Veterinarian:	HOOF ANGLES			HOOF LENGTHS		
		Left	Right		Left	Right
Trainer:	Front			Front		
	Back			Back		

Health Concerns:	Supplements:	Shoe Size:
		Shoe Type:
		Shoe Pads:
Therapeutic Treatments:	Special Requirements:	Dates Due:
Notes (Problems, Consultations, Changes, etc.):		Stable Name / Address:

CLIENT INFORMATION	Name:						
	Address:						
	Phone:			Email:			
HORSE INFORMATION	Name:			Breed:			
	Gender:			Primary Use:			
	Age:			Temperament (1-10):			

Veterinarian:	HOOF ANGLES			HOOF LENGTHS		
		Left	Right		Left	Right
Trainer:	Front			Front		
	Back			Back		
Health Concerns:	Supplements:			Shoe Size:		
				Shoe Type:		
				Shoe Pads:		
Therapeutic Treatments:	Special Requirements:			Dates Due:		
Notes (Problems, Consultations, Changes, etc.):				Stable Name / Address:		

CLIENT INFORMATION	Name:						
	Address:						
	Phone:			Email:			
HORSE INFORMATION	Name:			Breed:			
	Gender:			Primary Use:			
	Age:			Temperament (1-10):			

Veterinarian:	HOOF ANGLES			HOOF LENGTHS		
		Left	Right		Left	Right
Trainer:	Front			Front		
	Back			Back		
Health Concerns:	Supplements:			Shoe Size:		
				Shoe Type:		
				Shoe Pads:		
Therapeutic Treatments:	Special Requirements:			Dates Due:		
Notes (Problems, Consultations, Changes, etc.):				Stable Name / Address:		

CLIENT INFORMATION	Name:						
	Address:						
	Phone:			Email:			
HORSE INFORMATION	Name:			Breed:			
	Gender:			Primary Use:			
	Age:			Temperament (1-10):			

Veterinarian:	HOOF ANGLES			HOOF LENGTHS			
		Left	Right			Left	Right
Trainer:	Front				Front		
	Back				Back		
Health Concerns:	Supplements:			Shoe Size:			
				Shoe Type:			
				Shoe Pads:			
Therapeutic Treatments:	Special Requirements:			Dates Due:			
Notes (Problems, Consultations, Changes, etc.):				Stable Name / Address:			

CLIENT INFORMATION	Name:						
	Address:						
	Phone:			Email:			
HORSE INFORMATION	Name:			Breed:			
	Gender:			Primary Use:			
	Age:			Temperament (1-10):			

Veterinarian:	HOOF ANGLES			HOOF LENGTHS			
		Left	Right			Left	Right
Trainer:	Front				Front		
	Back				Back		
Health Concerns:	Supplements:			Shoe Size:			
				Shoe Type:			
				Shoe Pads:			
Therapeutic Treatments:	Special Requirements:			Dates Due:			
Notes (Problems, Consultations, Changes, etc.):				Stable Name / Address:			

CLIENT INFORMATION	Name:		
	Address:		
	Phone:	Email:	

HORSE INFORMATION	Name:	Breed:	
	Gender:	Primary Use:	
	Age:	Temperament (1-10):	

Veterinarian:	HOOF ANGLES			HOOF LENGTHS		
		Left	Right		Left	Right
Trainer:	Front			Front		
	Back			Back		
Health Concerns:	Supplements:			Shoe Size:		
				Shoe Type:		
				Shoe Pads:		
Therapeutic Treatments:	Special Requirements:			Dates Due:		
Notes (Problems, Consultations, Changes, etc.):				Stable Name / Address:		

CLIENT INFORMATION	Name:		
	Address:		
	Phone:	Email:	

HORSE INFORMATION	Name:	Breed:	
	Gender:	Primary Use:	
	Age:	Temperament (1-10):	

Veterinarian:	HOOF ANGLES			HOOF LENGTHS		
		Left	Right		Left	Right
Trainer:	Front			Front		
	Back			Back		
Health Concerns:	Supplements:			Shoe Size:		
				Shoe Type:		
				Shoe Pads:		
Therapeutic Treatments:	Special Requirements:			Dates Due:		
Notes (Problems, Consultations, Changes, etc.):				Stable Name / Address:		

CLIENT INFORMATION	Name:	
	Address:	
	Phone:	Email:

HORSE INFORMATION	Name:	Breed:
	Gender:	Primary Use:
	Age:	Temperament (1-10):

Veterinarian:	HOOF ANGLES			HOOF LENGTHS		
		Left	Right		Left	Right
Trainer:	Front			Front		
	Back			Back		
Health Concerns:	Supplements:			Shoe Size:		
				Shoe Type:		
				Shoe Pads:		
Therapeutic Treatments:	Special Requirements:			Dates Due:		
Notes (Problems, Consultations, Changes, etc.):				Stable Name / Address:		

CLIENT INFORMATION	Name:	
	Address:	
	Phone:	Email:

HORSE INFORMATION	Name:	Breed:
	Gender:	Primary Use:
	Age:	Temperament (1-10):

Veterinarian:	HOOF ANGLES			HOOF LENGTHS		
		Left	Right		Left	Right
Trainer:	Front			Front		
	Back			Back		
Health Concerns:	Supplements:			Shoe Size:		
				Shoe Type:		
				Shoe Pads:		
Therapeutic Treatments:	Special Requirements:			Dates Due:		
Notes (Problems, Consultations, Changes, etc.):				Stable Name / Address:		

CLIENT INFORMATION	Name:					
	Address:					
	Phone:			Email:		

HORSE INFORMATION	Name:			Breed:		
	Gender:			Primary Use:		
	Age:			Temperament (1-10):		

Veterinarian:	HOOF ANGLES			HOOF LENGTHS		
		Left	Right		Left	Right
Trainer:	Front			Front		
	Back			Back		
Health Concerns:	Supplements:			Shoe Size:		
				Shoe Type:		
				Shoe Pads:		
Therapeutic Treatments:	Special Requirements:			Dates Due:		
Notes (Problems, Consultations, Changes, etc.):				Stable Name / Address:		

CLIENT INFORMATION	Name:					
	Address:					
	Phone:			Email:		

HORSE INFORMATION	Name:			Breed:		
	Gender:			Primary Use:		
	Age:			Temperament (1-10):		

Veterinarian:	HOOF ANGLES			HOOF LENGTHS		
		Left	Right		Left	Right
Trainer:	Front			Front		
	Back			Back		
Health Concerns:	Supplements:			Shoe Size:		
				Shoe Type:		
				Shoe Pads:		
Therapeutic Treatments:	Special Requirements:			Dates Due:		
Notes (Problems, Consultations, Changes, etc.):				Stable Name / Address:		

CLIENT INFORMATION	Name:			
	Address:			
	Phone:		Email:	

HORSE INFORMATION	Name:		Breed:	
	Gender:		Primary Use:	
	Age:		Temperament (1-10):	

Veterinarian:	HOOF ANGLES			HOOF LENGTHS		
		Left	Right		Left	Right
Trainer:	Front			Front		
	Back			Back		

Health Concerns:	Supplements:	Shoe Size:
		Shoe Type:
		Shoe Pads:
Therapeutic Treatments:	Special Requirements:	Dates Due:
Notes (Problems, Consultations, Changes, etc.):		Stable Name / Address:

CLIENT INFORMATION	Name:			
	Address:			
	Phone:		Email:	

HORSE INFORMATION	Name:		Breed:	
	Gender:		Primary Use:	
	Age:		Temperament (1-10):	

Veterinarian:	HOOF ANGLES			HOOF LENGTHS		
		Left	Right		Left	Right
Trainer:	Front			Front		
	Back			Back		

Health Concerns:	Supplements:	Shoe Size:
		Shoe Type:
		Shoe Pads:
Therapeutic Treatments:	Special Requirements:	Dates Due:
Notes (Problems, Consultations, Changes, etc.):		Stable Name / Address:

CLIENT INFORMATION	Name:						
	Address:						
	Phone:			Email:			
HORSE INFORMATION	Name:			Breed:			
	Gender:			Primary Use:			
	Age:			Temperament (1-10):			

Veterinarian:	HOOF ANGLES			HOOF LENGTHS		
		Left	Right		Left	Right
Trainer:	Front			Front		
	Back			Back		
Health Concerns:	Supplements:			Shoe Size:		
				Shoe Type:		
				Shoe Pads:		
Therapeutic Treatments:	Special Requirements:			Dates Due:		
Notes (Problems, Consultations, Changes, etc.):				Stable Name / Address:		

CLIENT INFORMATION	Name:						
	Address:						
	Phone:			Email:			
HORSE INFORMATION	Name:			Breed:			
	Gender:			Primary Use:			
	Age:			Temperament (1-10):			

Veterinarian:	HOOF ANGLES			HOOF LENGTHS		
		Left	Right		Left	Right
Trainer:	Front			Front		
	Back			Back		
Health Concerns:	Supplements:			Shoe Size:		
				Shoe Type:		
				Shoe Pads:		
Therapeutic Treatments:	Special Requirements:			Dates Due:		
Notes (Problems, Consultations, Changes, etc.):				Stable Name / Address:		

CLIENT INFORMATION	Name:		
	Address:		
	Phone:		Email:

HORSE INFORMATION	Name:		Breed:
	Gender:		Primary Use:
	Age:		Temperament (1-10):

Veterinarian:	HOOF ANGLES			HOOF LENGTHS		
		Left	Right		Left	Right
Trainer:	Front			Front		
	Back			Back		

Health Concerns:	Supplements:	Shoe Size:
		Shoe Type:
		Shoe Pads:
Therapeutic Treatments:	Special Requirements:	Dates Due:

| Notes (Problems, Consultations, Changes, etc.): | Stable Name / Address: |

CLIENT INFORMATION	Name:		
	Address:		
	Phone:		Email:

HORSE INFORMATION	Name:		Breed:
	Gender:		Primary Use:
	Age:		Temperament (1-10):

Veterinarian:	HOOF ANGLES			HOOF LENGTHS		
		Left	Right		Left	Right
Trainer:	Front			Front		
	Back			Back		

Health Concerns:	Supplements:	Shoe Size:
		Shoe Type:
		Shoe Pads:
Therapeutic Treatments:	Special Requirements:	Dates Due:

| Notes (Problems, Consultations, Changes, etc.): | Stable Name / Address: |

CLIENT INFORMATION	Name:						
	Address:						
	Phone:			Email:			
HORSE INFORMATION	Name:			Breed:			
	Gender:			Primary Use:			
	Age:			Temperament (1-10):			

Veterinarian:	HOOF ANGLES			HOOF LENGTHS		
		Left	Right		Left	Right
Trainer:	Front			Front		
	Back			Back		
Health Concerns:	Supplements:			Shoe Size:		
				Shoe Type:		
				Shoe Pads:		
Therapeutic Treatments:	Special Requirements:			Dates Due:		
Notes (Problems, Consultations, Changes, etc.):				Stable Name / Address:		

CLIENT INFORMATION	Name:						
	Address:						
	Phone:			Email:			
HORSE INFORMATION	Name:			Breed:			
	Gender:			Primary Use:			
	Age:			Temperament (1-10):			

Veterinarian:	HOOF ANGLES			HOOF LENGTHS		
		Left	Right		Left	Right
Trainer:	Front			Front		
	Back			Back		
Health Concerns:	Supplements:			Shoe Size:		
				Shoe Type:		
				Shoe Pads:		
Therapeutic Treatments:	Special Requirements:			Dates Due:		
Notes (Problems, Consultations, Changes, etc.):				Stable Name / Address:		

CLIENT INFORMATION	Name:					
	Address:					
	Phone:			Email:		
HORSE INFORMATION	Name:			Breed:		
	Gender:			Primary Use:		
	Age:			Temperament (1-10):		
Veterinarian:	HOOF ANGLES			HOOF LENGTHS		
		Left	Right		Left	Right
Trainer:	Front			Front		
	Back			Back		
Health Concerns:	Supplements:			Shoe Size:		
				Shoe Type:		
				Shoe Pads:		
Therapeutic Treatments:	Special Requirements:			Dates Due:		
Notes (Problems, Consultations, Changes, etc.):				Stable Name / Address:		

CLIENT INFORMATION	Name:					
	Address:					
	Phone:			Email:		
HORSE INFORMATION	Name:			Breed:		
	Gender:			Primary Use:		
	Age:			Temperament (1-10):		
Veterinarian:	HOOF ANGLES			HOOF LENGTHS		
		Left	Right		Left	Right
Trainer:	Front			Front		
	Back			Back		
Health Concerns:	Supplements:			Shoe Size:		
				Shoe Type:		
				Shoe Pads:		
Therapeutic Treatments:	Special Requirements:			Dates Due:		
Notes (Problems, Consultations, Changes, etc.):				Stable Name / Address:		

CLIENT INFORMATION	Name:		
	Address:		
	Phone:		Email:

HORSE INFORMATION	Name:		Breed:
	Gender:		Primary Use:
	Age:		Temperament (1-10):

Veterinarian:	HOOF ANGLES			HOOF LENGTHS		
		Left	Right		Left	Right
Trainer:	Front			Front		
	Back			Back		
Health Concerns:	Supplements:			Shoe Size:		
				Shoe Type:		
				Shoe Pads:		
Therapeutic Treatments:	Special Requirements:			Dates Due:		
Notes (Problems, Consultations, Changes, etc.):				Stable Name / Address:		

CLIENT INFORMATION	Name:		
	Address:		
	Phone:		Email:

HORSE INFORMATION	Name:		Breed:
	Gender:		Primary Use:
	Age:		Temperament (1-10):

Veterinarian:	HOOF ANGLES			HOOF LENGTHS		
		Left	Right		Left	Right
Trainer:	Front			Front		
	Back			Back		
Health Concerns:	Supplements:			Shoe Size:		
				Shoe Type:		
				Shoe Pads:		
Therapeutic Treatments:	Special Requirements:			Dates Due:		
Notes (Problems, Consultations, Changes, etc.):				Stable Name / Address:		

CLIENT INFORMATION	Name:		
	Address:		
	Phone:	Email:	

HORSE INFORMATION	Name:	Breed:	
	Gender:	Primary Use:	
	Age:	Temperament (1-10):	

Veterinarian:	HOOF ANGLES			HOOF LENGTHS		
		Left	Right		Left	Right
Trainer:	Front			Front		
	Back			Back		

Health Concerns:	Supplements:	Shoe Size:
		Shoe Type:
		Shoe Pads:
Therapeutic Treatments:	Special Requirements:	Dates Due:

Notes (Problems, Consultations, Changes, etc.):	Stable Name / Address:

CLIENT INFORMATION	Name:		
	Address:		
	Phone:	Email:	

HORSE INFORMATION	Name:	Breed:	
	Gender:	Primary Use:	
	Age:	Temperament (1-10):	

Veterinarian:	HOOF ANGLES			HOOF LENGTHS		
		Left	Right		Left	Right
Trainer:	Front			Front		
	Back			Back		

Health Concerns:	Supplements:	Shoe Size:
		Shoe Type:
		Shoe Pads:
Therapeutic Treatments:	Special Requirements:	Dates Due:

Notes (Problems, Consultations, Changes, etc.):	Stable Name / Address:

CLIENT INFORMATION	Name:	
	Address:	
	Phone:	Email:

HORSE INFORMATION	Name:	Breed:
	Gender:	Primary Use:
	Age:	Temperament (1-10):

Veterinarian:	HOOF ANGLES			HOOF LENGTHS		
		Left	Right		Left	Right
Trainer:	Front			Front		
	Back			Back		
Health Concerns:	Supplements:			Shoe Size:		
				Shoe Type:		
				Shoe Pads:		
Therapeutic Treatments:	Special Requirements:			Dates Due:		
Notes (Problems, Consultations, Changes, etc.):				Stable Name / Address:		

CLIENT INFORMATION	Name:	
	Address:	
	Phone:	Email:

HORSE INFORMATION	Name:	Breed:
	Gender:	Primary Use:
	Age:	Temperament (1-10):

Veterinarian:	HOOF ANGLES			HOOF LENGTHS		
		Left	Right		Left	Right
Trainer:	Front			Front		
	Back			Back		
Health Concerns:	Supplements:			Shoe Size:		
				Shoe Type:		
				Shoe Pads:		
Therapeutic Treatments:	Special Requirements:			Dates Due:		
Notes (Problems, Consultations, Changes, etc.):				Stable Name / Address:		

CLIENT INFORMATION	Name:						
	Address:						
	Phone:			Email:			
HORSE INFORMATION	Name:			Breed:			
	Gender:			Primary Use:			
	Age:			Temperament (1-10):			
Veterinarian:	HOOF ANGLES			HOOF LENGTHS			
		Left	Right			Left	Right
Trainer:	Front				Front		
	Back				Back		
Health Concerns:	Supplements:			Shoe Size:			
				Shoe Type:			
				Shoe Pads:			
Therapeutic Treatments:	Special Requirements:			Dates Due:			
Notes (Problems, Consultations, Changes, etc.):				Stable Name / Address:			

CLIENT INFORMATION	Name:						
	Address:						
	Phone:			Email:			
HORSE INFORMATION	Name:			Breed:			
	Gender:			Primary Use:			
	Age:			Temperament (1-10):			
Veterinarian:	HOOF ANGLES			HOOF LENGTHS			
		Left	Right			Left	Right
Trainer:	Front				Front		
	Back				Back		
Health Concerns:	Supplements:			Shoe Size:			
				Shoe Type:			
				Shoe Pads:			
Therapeutic Treatments:	Special Requirements:			Dates Due:			
Notes (Problems, Consultations, Changes, etc.):				Stable Name / Address:			

CLIENT INFORMATION	Name:	
	Address:	
	Phone:	Email:
HORSE INFORMATION	Name:	Breed:
	Gender:	Primary Use:
	Age:	Temperament (1-10):

Veterinarian:	HOOF ANGLES			HOOF LENGTHS		
		Left	Right		Left	Right
Trainer:	Front			Front		
	Back			Back		

Health Concerns:	Supplements:	Shoe Size:
		Shoe Type:
		Shoe Pads:
Therapeutic Treatments:	Special Requirements:	Dates Due:
Notes (Problems, Consultations, Changes, etc.):		Stable Name / Address:

CLIENT INFORMATION	Name:	
	Address:	
	Phone:	Email:
HORSE INFORMATION	Name:	Breed:
	Gender:	Primary Use:
	Age:	Temperament (1-10):

Veterinarian:	HOOF ANGLES			HOOF LENGTHS		
		Left	Right		Left	Right
Trainer:	Front			Front		
	Back			Back		

Health Concerns:	Supplements:	Shoe Size:
		Shoe Type:
		Shoe Pads:
Therapeutic Treatments:	Special Requirements:	Dates Due:
Notes (Problems, Consultations, Changes, etc.):		Stable Name / Address:

CLIENT INFORMATION	Name:						
	Address:						
	Phone:			Email:			
HORSE INFORMATION	Name:			Breed:			
	Gender:			Primary Use:			
	Age:			Temperament (1-10):			

Veterinarian:	HOOF ANGLES			HOOF LENGTHS		
		Left	Right		Left	Right
Trainer:	Front			Front		
	Back			Back		
Health Concerns:	Supplements:			Shoe Size:		
				Shoe Type:		
				Shoe Pads:		
Therapeutic Treatments:	Special Requirements:			Dates Due:		
Notes (Problems, Consultations, Changes, etc.):				Stable Name / Address:		

CLIENT INFORMATION	Name:						
	Address:						
	Phone:			Email:			
HORSE INFORMATION	Name:			Breed:			
	Gender:			Primary Use:			
	Age:			Temperament (1-10):			

Veterinarian:	HOOF ANGLES			HOOF LENGTHS		
		Left	Right		Left	Right
Trainer:	Front			Front		
	Back			Back		
Health Concerns:	Supplements:			Shoe Size:		
				Shoe Type:		
				Shoe Pads:		
Therapeutic Treatments:	Special Requirements:			Dates Due:		
Notes (Problems, Consultations, Changes, etc.):				Stable Name / Address:		

CLIENT INFORMATION	Name:						
	Address:						
	Phone:			Email:			
HORSE INFORMATION	Name:			Breed:			
	Gender:			Primary Use:			
	Age:			Temperament (1-10):			

Veterinarian:	HOOF ANGLES			HOOF LENGTHS		
		Left	Right		Left	Right
Trainer:	Front			Front		
	Back			Back		

Health Concerns:	Supplements:	Shoe Size:
		Shoe Type:
		Shoe Pads:
Therapeutic Treatments:	Special Requirements:	Dates Due:
Notes (Problems, Consultations, Changes, etc.):		Stable Name / Address:

CLIENT INFORMATION	Name:						
	Address:						
	Phone:			Email:			
HORSE INFORMATION	Name:			Breed:			
	Gender:			Primary Use:			
	Age:			Temperament (1-10):			

Veterinarian:	HOOF ANGLES			HOOF LENGTHS		
		Left	Right		Left	Right
Trainer:	Front			Front		
	Back			Back		

Health Concerns:	Supplements:	Shoe Size:
		Shoe Type:
		Shoe Pads:
Therapeutic Treatments:	Special Requirements:	Dates Due:
Notes (Problems, Consultations, Changes, etc.):		Stable Name / Address:

CLIENT INFORMATION	Name:	
	Address:	
	Phone:	Email:

HORSE INFORMATION	Name:	Breed:
	Gender:	Primary Use:
	Age:	Temperament (1-10):

Veterinarian:	HOOF ANGLES			HOOF LENGTHS		
		Left	Right		Left	Right
Trainer:	Front			Front		
	Back			Back		

Health Concerns:	Supplements:	Shoe Size:
		Shoe Type:
		Shoe Pads:
Therapeutic Treatments:	Special Requirements:	Dates Due:

Notes (Problems, Consultations, Changes, etc.):	Stable Name / Address:

CLIENT INFORMATION	Name:	
	Address:	
	Phone:	Email:

HORSE INFORMATION	Name:	Breed:
	Gender:	Primary Use:
	Age:	Temperament (1-10):

Veterinarian:	HOOF ANGLES			HOOF LENGTHS		
		Left	Right		Left	Right
Trainer:	Front			Front		
	Back			Back		

Health Concerns:	Supplements:	Shoe Size:
		Shoe Type:
		Shoe Pads:
Therapeutic Treatments:	Special Requirements:	Dates Due:

Notes (Problems, Consultations, Changes, etc.):	Stable Name / Address:

CLIENT INFORMATION	Name:					
	Address:					
	Phone:			Email:		
HORSE INFORMATION	Name:			Breed:		
	Gender:			Primary Use:		
	Age:			Temperament (1-10):		

Veterinarian:	HOOF ANGLES			HOOF LENGTHS		
		Left	Right		Left	Right
Trainer:	Front			Front		
	Back			Back		
Health Concerns:	Supplements:			Shoe Size:		
				Shoe Type:		
				Shoe Pads:		
Therapeutic Treatments:	Special Requirements:			Dates Due:		
Notes (Problems, Consultations, Changes, etc.):				Stable Name / Address:		

CLIENT INFORMATION	Name:					
	Address:					
	Phone:			Email:		
HORSE INFORMATION	Name:			Breed:		
	Gender:			Primary Use:		
	Age:			Temperament (1-10):		

Veterinarian:	HOOF ANGLES			HOOF LENGTHS		
		Left	Right		Left	Right
Trainer:	Front			Front		
	Back			Back		
Health Concerns:	Supplements:			Shoe Size:		
				Shoe Type:		
				Shoe Pads:		
Therapeutic Treatments:	Special Requirements:			Dates Due:		
Notes (Problems, Consultations, Changes, etc.):				Stable Name / Address:		

CLIENT INFORMATION	Name:		
	Address:		
	Phone:		Email:

HORSE INFORMATION	Name:		Breed:
	Gender:		Primary Use:
	Age:		Temperament (1-10):

Veterinarian:	HOOF ANGLES			HOOF LENGTHS		
		Left	Right		Left	Right
Trainer:	Front			Front		
	Back			Back		

Health Concerns:	Supplements:	Shoe Size:
		Shoe Type:
		Shoe Pads:
Therapeutic Treatments:	Special Requirements:	Dates Due:
Notes (Problems, Consultations, Changes, etc.):		Stable Name / Address:

CLIENT INFORMATION	Name:		
	Address:		
	Phone:		Email:

HORSE INFORMATION	Name:		Breed:
	Gender:		Primary Use:
	Age:		Temperament (1-10):

Veterinarian:	HOOF ANGLES			HOOF LENGTHS		
		Left	Right		Left	Right
Trainer:	Front			Front		
	Back			Back		

Health Concerns:	Supplements:	Shoe Size:
		Shoe Type:
		Shoe Pads:
Therapeutic Treatments:	Special Requirements:	Dates Due:
Notes (Problems, Consultations, Changes, etc.):		Stable Name / Address:

CLIENT INFORMATION	Name:						
	Address:						
	Phone:			Email:			

HORSE INFORMATION	Name:			Breed:			
	Gender:			Primary Use:			
	Age:			Temperament (1-10):			

Veterinarian:	HOOF ANGLES			HOOF LENGTHS			
		Left	Right			Left	Right
Trainer:	Front				Front		
	Back				Back		
Health Concerns:	Supplements:			Shoe Size:			
				Shoe Type:			
				Shoe Pads:			
Therapeutic Treatments:	Special Requirements:			Dates Due:			
Notes (Problems, Consultations, Changes, etc.):				Stable Name / Address:			

CLIENT INFORMATION	Name:						
	Address:						
	Phone:			Email:			

HORSE INFORMATION	Name:			Breed:			
	Gender:			Primary Use:			
	Age:			Temperament (1-10):			

Veterinarian:	HOOF ANGLES			HOOF LENGTHS			
		Left	Right			Left	Right
Trainer:	Front				Front		
	Back				Back		
Health Concerns:	Supplements:			Shoe Size:			
				Shoe Type:			
				Shoe Pads:			
Therapeutic Treatments:	Special Requirements:			Dates Due:			
Notes (Problems, Consultations, Changes, etc.):				Stable Name / Address:			

CLIENT INFORMATION	Name:				
	Address:				
	Phone:			Email:	

HORSE INFORMATION	Name:			Breed:	
	Gender:			Primary Use:	
	Age:			Temperament (1-10):	

Veterinarian:	HOOF ANGLES			HOOF LENGTHS		
		Left	Right		Left	Right
Trainer:	Front			Front		
	Back			Back		

Health Concerns:	Supplements:	Shoe Size:
		Shoe Type:
		Shoe Pads:
Therapeutic Treatments:	Special Requirements:	Dates Due:
Notes (Problems, Consultations, Changes, etc.):		Stable Name / Address:

CLIENT INFORMATION	Name:				
	Address:				
	Phone:			Email:	

HORSE INFORMATION	Name:			Breed:	
	Gender:			Primary Use:	
	Age:			Temperament (1-10):	

Veterinarian:	HOOF ANGLES			HOOF LENGTHS		
		Left	Right		Left	Right
Trainer:	Front			Front		
	Back			Back		

Health Concerns:	Supplements:	Shoe Size:
		Shoe Type:
		Shoe Pads:
Therapeutic Treatments:	Special Requirements:	Dates Due:
Notes (Problems, Consultations, Changes, etc.):		Stable Name / Address:

CLIENT INFORMATION	Name:		
	Address:		
	Phone:		Email:

HORSE INFORMATION	Name:		Breed:
	Gender:		Primary Use:
	Age:		Temperament (1-10):

Veterinarian:	HOOF ANGLES			HOOF LENGTHS		
		Left	Right		Left	Right
Trainer:	Front			Front		
	Back			Back		

Health Concerns:	Supplements:	Shoe Size:
		Shoe Type:
		Shoe Pads:
Therapeutic Treatments:	Special Requirements:	Dates Due:

| Notes (Problems, Consultations, Changes, etc.): | Stable Name / Address: |

CLIENT INFORMATION	Name:		
	Address:		
	Phone:		Email:

HORSE INFORMATION	Name:		Breed:
	Gender:		Primary Use:
	Age:		Temperament (1-10):

Veterinarian:	HOOF ANGLES			HOOF LENGTHS		
		Left	Right		Left	Right
Trainer:	Front			Front		
	Back			Back		

Health Concerns:	Supplements:	Shoe Size:
		Shoe Type:
		Shoe Pads:
Therapeutic Treatments:	Special Requirements:	Dates Due:

| Notes (Problems, Consultations, Changes, etc.): | Stable Name / Address: |

CLIENT INFORMATION	Name:		
	Address:		
	Phone:		Email:
HORSE INFORMATION	Name:		Breed:
	Gender:		Primary Use:
	Age:		Temperament (1-10):

Veterinarian:	HOOF ANGLES			HOOF LENGTHS		
		Left	Right		Left	Right
Trainer:	Front			Front		
	Back			Back		

Health Concerns:	Supplements:	Shoe Size:
		Shoe Type:
		Shoe Pads:
Therapeutic Treatments:	Special Requirements:	Dates Due:
Notes (Problems, Consultations, Changes, etc.):		Stable Name / Address:

CLIENT INFORMATION	Name:		
	Address:		
	Phone:		Email:
HORSE INFORMATION	Name:		Breed:
	Gender:		Primary Use:
	Age:		Temperament (1-10):

Veterinarian:	HOOF ANGLES			HOOF LENGTHS		
		Left	Right		Left	Right
Trainer:	Front			Front		
	Back			Back		

Health Concerns:	Supplements:	Shoe Size:
		Shoe Type:
		Shoe Pads:
Therapeutic Treatments:	Special Requirements:	Dates Due:
Notes (Problems, Consultations, Changes, etc.):		Stable Name / Address:

CLIENT INFORMATION	Name:						
	Address:						
	Phone:			Email:			
HORSE INFORMATION	Name:			Breed:			
	Gender:			Primary Use:			
	Age:			Temperament (1-10):			

Veterinarian:	HOOF ANGLES			HOOF LENGTHS		
		Left	Right		Left	Right
Trainer:	Front			Front		
	Back			Back		

Health Concerns:	Supplements:	Shoe Size:
		Shoe Type:
		Shoe Pads:
Therapeutic Treatments:	Special Requirements:	Dates Due:
Notes (Problems, Consultations, Changes, etc.):		Stable Name / Address:

CLIENT INFORMATION	Name:						
	Address:						
	Phone:			Email:			
HORSE INFORMATION	Name:			Breed:			
	Gender:			Primary Use:			
	Age:			Temperament (1-10):			

Veterinarian:	HOOF ANGLES			HOOF LENGTHS		
		Left	Right		Left	Right
Trainer:	Front			Front		
	Back			Back		

Health Concerns:	Supplements:	Shoe Size:
		Shoe Type:
		Shoe Pads:
Therapeutic Treatments:	Special Requirements:	Dates Due:
Notes (Problems, Consultations, Changes, etc.):		Stable Name / Address:

Form 1

CLIENT INFORMATION	Name:	
	Address:	
	Phone:	Email:

HORSE INFORMATION	Name:	Breed:
	Gender:	Primary Use:
	Age:	Temperament (1-10):

Veterinarian:	HOOF ANGLES			HOOF LENGTHS		
		Left	Right		Left	Right
Trainer:	Front			Front		
	Back			Back		

Health Concerns:	Supplements:	Shoe Size:
		Shoe Type:
		Shoe Pads:
Therapeutic Treatments:	Special Requirements:	Dates Due:

Notes (Problems, Consultations, Changes, etc.):	Stable Name / Address:

Form 2

CLIENT INFORMATION	Name:	
	Address:	
	Phone:	Email:

HORSE INFORMATION	Name:	Breed:
	Gender:	Primary Use:
	Age:	Temperament (1-10):

Veterinarian:	HOOF ANGLES			HOOF LENGTHS		
		Left	Right		Left	Right
Trainer:	Front			Front		
	Back			Back		

Health Concerns:	Supplements:	Shoe Size:
		Shoe Type:
		Shoe Pads:
Therapeutic Treatments:	Special Requirements:	Dates Due:

Notes (Problems, Consultations, Changes, etc.):	Stable Name / Address:

CLIENT INFORMATION	Name:						
	Address:						
	Phone:			Email:			
HORSE INFORMATION	Name:			Breed:			
	Gender:			Primary Use:			
	Age:			Temperament (1-10):			

Veterinarian:	HOOF ANGLES			HOOF LENGTHS		
		Left	Right		Left	Right
Trainer:	Front			Front		
	Back			Back		
Health Concerns:	Supplements:			Shoe Size:		
				Shoe Type:		
				Shoe Pads:		
Therapeutic Treatments:	Special Requirements:			Dates Due:		
Notes (Problems, Consultations, Changes, etc.):				Stable Name / Address:		

CLIENT INFORMATION	Name:						
	Address:						
	Phone:			Email:			
HORSE INFORMATION	Name:			Breed:			
	Gender:			Primary Use:			
	Age:			Temperament (1-10):			

Veterinarian:	HOOF ANGLES			HOOF LENGTHS		
		Left	Right		Left	Right
Trainer:	Front			Front		
	Back			Back		
Health Concerns:	Supplements:			Shoe Size:		
				Shoe Type:		
				Shoe Pads:		
Therapeutic Treatments:	Special Requirements:			Dates Due:		
Notes (Problems, Consultations, Changes, etc.):				Stable Name / Address:		

CLIENT INFORMATION	Name:		
	Address:		
	Phone:	Email:	

HORSE INFORMATION	Name:	Breed:	
	Gender:	Primary Use:	
	Age:	Temperament (1-10):	

Veterinarian:	HOOF ANGLES			HOOF LENGTHS		
		Left	Right		Left	Right
Trainer:	Front			Front		
	Back			Back		

Health Concerns:	Supplements:	Shoe Size:
		Shoe Type:
		Shoe Pads:
Therapeutic Treatments:	Special Requirements:	Dates Due:
Notes (Problems, Consultations, Changes, etc.):		Stable Name / Address:

CLIENT INFORMATION	Name:		
	Address:		
	Phone:	Email:	

HORSE INFORMATION	Name:	Breed:	
	Gender:	Primary Use:	
	Age:	Temperament (1-10):	

Veterinarian:	HOOF ANGLES			HOOF LENGTHS		
		Left	Right		Left	Right
Trainer:	Front			Front		
	Back			Back		

Health Concerns:	Supplements:	Shoe Size:
		Shoe Type:
		Shoe Pads:
Therapeutic Treatments:	Special Requirements:	Dates Due:
Notes (Problems, Consultations, Changes, etc.):		Stable Name / Address:

CLIENT INFORMATION	Name:					
	Address:					
	Phone:			Email:		

HORSE INFORMATION	Name:			Breed:		
	Gender:			Primary Use:		
	Age:			Temperament (1-10):		

Veterinarian:	HOOF ANGLES			HOOF LENGTHS		
		Left	Right		Left	Right
Trainer:	Front			Front		
	Back			Back		
Health Concerns:	Supplements:			Shoe Size:		
				Shoe Type:		
				Shoe Pads:		
Therapeutic Treatments:	Special Requirements:			Dates Due:		
Notes (Problems, Consultations, Changes, etc.):				Stable Name / Address:		

CLIENT INFORMATION	Name:					
	Address:					
	Phone:			Email:		

HORSE INFORMATION	Name:			Breed:		
	Gender:			Primary Use:		
	Age:			Temperament (1-10):		

Veterinarian:	HOOF ANGLES			HOOF LENGTHS		
		Left	Right		Left	Right
Trainer:	Front			Front		
	Back			Back		
Health Concerns:	Supplements:			Shoe Size:		
				Shoe Type:		
				Shoe Pads:		
Therapeutic Treatments:	Special Requirements:			Dates Due:		
Notes (Problems, Consultations, Changes, etc.):				Stable Name / Address:		

CLIENT INFORMATION	Name:		
	Address:		
	Phone:		Email:

HORSE INFORMATION	Name:		Breed:
	Gender:		Primary Use:
	Age:		Temperament (1-10):

Veterinarian:	HOOF ANGLES			HOOF LENGTHS		
		Left	Right		Left	Right
Trainer:	Front			Front		
	Back			Back		

Health Concerns:	Supplements:	Shoe Size:
		Shoe Type:
		Shoe Pads:
Therapeutic Treatments:	Special Requirements:	Dates Due:
Notes (Problems, Consultations, Changes, etc.):		Stable Name / Address:

CLIENT INFORMATION	Name:		
	Address:		
	Phone:		Email:

HORSE INFORMATION	Name:		Breed:
	Gender:		Primary Use:
	Age:		Temperament (1-10):

Veterinarian:	HOOF ANGLES			HOOF LENGTHS		
		Left	Right		Left	Right
Trainer:	Front			Front		
	Back			Back		

Health Concerns:	Supplements:	Shoe Size:
		Shoe Type:
		Shoe Pads:
Therapeutic Treatments:	Special Requirements:	Dates Due:
Notes (Problems, Consultations, Changes, etc.):		Stable Name / Address:

CLIENT INFORMATION	Name:		
	Address:		
	Phone:		Email:
HORSE INFORMATION	Name:		Breed:
	Gender:		Primary Use:
	Age:		Temperament (1-10):

Veterinarian:	HOOF ANGLES			HOOF LENGTHS		
		Left	Right		Left	Right
Trainer:	Front			Front		
	Back			Back		
Health Concerns:	Supplements:			Shoe Size:		
				Shoe Type:		
				Shoe Pads:		
Therapeutic Treatments:	Special Requirements:			Dates Due:		
Notes (Problems, Consultations, Changes, etc.):				Stable Name / Address:		

CLIENT INFORMATION	Name:		
	Address:		
	Phone:		Email:
HORSE INFORMATION	Name:		Breed:
	Gender:		Primary Use:
	Age:		Temperament (1-10):

Veterinarian:	HOOF ANGLES			HOOF LENGTHS		
		Left	Right		Left	Right
Trainer:	Front			Front		
	Back			Back		
Health Concerns:	Supplements:			Shoe Size:		
				Shoe Type:		
				Shoe Pads:		
Therapeutic Treatments:	Special Requirements:			Dates Due:		
Notes (Problems, Consultations, Changes, etc.):				Stable Name / Address:		

CLIENT INFORMATION	Name:			
	Address:			
	Phone:		Email:	

HORSE INFORMATION	Name:		Breed:	
	Gender:		Primary Use:	
	Age:		Temperament (1-10):	

Veterinarian:	HOOF ANGLES			HOOF LENGTHS		
		Left	Right		Left	Right
Trainer:	Front			Front		
	Back			Back		

Health Concerns:	Supplements:	Shoe Size:
		Shoe Type:
		Shoe Pads:
Therapeutic Treatments:	Special Requirements:	Dates Due:
Notes (Problems, Consultations, Changes, etc.):		Stable Name / Address:

CLIENT INFORMATION	Name:			
	Address:			
	Phone:		Email:	

HORSE INFORMATION	Name:		Breed:	
	Gender:		Primary Use:	
	Age:		Temperament (1-10):	

Veterinarian:	HOOF ANGLES			HOOF LENGTHS		
		Left	Right		Left	Right
Trainer:	Front			Front		
	Back			Back		

Health Concerns:	Supplements:	Shoe Size:
		Shoe Type:
		Shoe Pads:
Therapeutic Treatments:	Special Requirements:	Dates Due:
Notes (Problems, Consultations, Changes, etc.):		Stable Name / Address:

CLIENT INFORMATION	Name:	
	Address:	
	Phone:	Email:
HORSE INFORMATION	Name:	Breed:
	Gender:	Primary Use:
	Age:	Temperament (1-10):

Veterinarian:	HOOF ANGLES			HOOF LENGTHS		
		Left	Right		Left	Right
Trainer:	Front			Front		
	Back			Back		
Health Concerns:	Supplements:			Shoe Size:		
				Shoe Type:		
				Shoe Pads:		
Therapeutic Treatments:	Special Requirements:			Dates Due:		
Notes (Problems, Consultations, Changes, etc.):				Stable Name / Address:		

CLIENT INFORMATION	Name:	
	Address:	
	Phone:	Email:
HORSE INFORMATION	Name:	Breed:
	Gender:	Primary Use:
	Age:	Temperament (1-10):

Veterinarian:	HOOF ANGLES			HOOF LENGTHS		
		Left	Right		Left	Right
Trainer:	Front			Front		
	Back			Back		
Health Concerns:	Supplements:			Shoe Size:		
				Shoe Type:		
				Shoe Pads:		
Therapeutic Treatments:	Special Requirements:			Dates Due:		
Notes (Problems, Consultations, Changes, etc.):				Stable Name / Address:		

CLIENT INFORMATION	Name:						
	Address:						
	Phone:			Email:			
HORSE INFORMATION	Name:			Breed:			
	Gender:			Primary Use:			
	Age:			Temperament (1-10):			

Veterinarian:	HOOF ANGLES			HOOF LENGTHS		
		Left	Right		Left	Right
Trainer:	Front			Front		
	Back			Back		

Health Concerns:	Supplements:	Shoe Size:
		Shoe Type:
		Shoe Pads:
Therapeutic Treatments:	Special Requirements:	Dates Due:
Notes (Problems, Consultations, Changes, etc.):		Stable Name / Address:

CLIENT INFORMATION	Name:						
	Address:						
	Phone:			Email:			
HORSE INFORMATION	Name:			Breed:			
	Gender:			Primary Use:			
	Age:			Temperament (1-10):			

Veterinarian:	HOOF ANGLES			HOOF LENGTHS		
		Left	Right		Left	Right
Trainer:	Front			Front		
	Back			Back		

Health Concerns:	Supplements:	Shoe Size:
		Shoe Type:
		Shoe Pads:
Therapeutic Treatments:	Special Requirements:	Dates Due:
Notes (Problems, Consultations, Changes, etc.):		Stable Name / Address:

CLIENT INFORMATION

Name:	
Address:	
Phone:	Email:

HORSE INFORMATION

Name:	Breed:
Gender:	Primary Use:
Age:	Temperament (1-10):

Veterinarian:

HOOF ANGLES			HOOF LENGTHS		
	Left	Right		Left	Right
Front			Front		
Back			Back		

Trainer:

Health Concerns:	Supplements:	Shoe Size:
		Shoe Type:
		Shoe Pads:
Therapeutic Treatments:	Special Requirements:	Dates Due:

Notes (Problems, Consultations, Changes, etc.):	Stable Name / Address:

CLIENT INFORMATION

Name:	
Address:	
Phone:	Email:

HORSE INFORMATION

Name:	Breed:
Gender:	Primary Use:
Age:	Temperament (1-10):

Veterinarian:

HOOF ANGLES			HOOF LENGTHS		
	Left	Right		Left	Right
Front			Front		
Back			Back		

Trainer:

Health Concerns:	Supplements:	Shoe Size:
		Shoe Type:
		Shoe Pads:
Therapeutic Treatments:	Special Requirements:	Dates Due:

Notes (Problems, Consultations, Changes, etc.):	Stable Name / Address:

CLIENT INFORMATION	Name:						
	Address:						
	Phone:			Email:			
HORSE INFORMATION	Name:			Breed:			
	Gender:			Primary Use:			
	Age:			Temperament (1-10):			
Veterinarian:	HOOF ANGLES			HOOF LENGTHS			
		Left	Right			Left	Right
Trainer:	Front				Front		
	Back				Back		
Health Concerns:	Supplements:			Shoe Size:			
				Shoe Type:			
				Shoe Pads:			
Therapeutic Treatments:	Special Requirements:			Dates Due:			
Notes (Problems, Consultations, Changes, etc.):				Stable Name / Address:			

CLIENT INFORMATION	Name:						
	Address:						
	Phone:			Email:			
HORSE INFORMATION	Name:			Breed:			
	Gender:			Primary Use:			
	Age:			Temperament (1-10):			
Veterinarian:	HOOF ANGLES			HOOF LENGTHS			
		Left	Right			Left	Right
Trainer:	Front				Front		
	Back				Back		
Health Concerns:	Supplements:			Shoe Size:			
				Shoe Type:			
				Shoe Pads:			
Therapeutic Treatments:	Special Requirements:			Dates Due:			
Notes (Problems, Consultations, Changes, etc.):				Stable Name / Address:			

CLIENT INFORMATION	Name:		
	Address:		
	Phone:		Email:
HORSE INFORMATION	Name:		Breed:
	Gender:		Primary Use:
	Age:		Temperament (1-10):

Veterinarian:	HOOF ANGLES			HOOF LENGTHS		
		Left	Right		Left	Right
Trainer:	Front			Front		
	Back			Back		
Health Concerns:	Supplements:		Shoe Size:		
			Shoe Type:		
			Shoe Pads:		
Therapeutic Treatments:	Special Requirements:		Dates Due:		
Notes (Problems, Consultations, Changes, etc.):			Stable Name / Address:		

CLIENT INFORMATION	Name:		
	Address:		
	Phone:		Email:
HORSE INFORMATION	Name:		Breed:
	Gender:		Primary Use:
	Age:		Temperament (1-10):

Veterinarian:	HOOF ANGLES			HOOF LENGTHS		
		Left	Right		Left	Right
Trainer:	Front			Front		
	Back			Back		
Health Concerns:	Supplements:		Shoe Size:		
			Shoe Type:		
			Shoe Pads:		
Therapeutic Treatments:	Special Requirements:		Dates Due:		
Notes (Problems, Consultations, Changes, etc.):			Stable Name / Address:		

CLIENT INFORMATION	Name:	
	Address:	
	Phone:	Email:

HORSE INFORMATION	Name:	Breed:
	Gender:	Primary Use:
	Age:	Temperament (1-10):

Veterinarian:	HOOF ANGLES			HOOF LENGTHS		
		Left	Right		Left	Right
Trainer:	Front			Front		
	Back			Back		
Health Concerns:	Supplements:			Shoe Size:		
				Shoe Type:		
				Shoe Pads:		
Therapeutic Treatments:	Special Requirements:			Dates Due:		
Notes (Problems, Consultations, Changes, etc.):				Stable Name / Address:		

CLIENT INFORMATION	Name:	
	Address:	
	Phone:	Email:

HORSE INFORMATION	Name:	Breed:
	Gender:	Primary Use:
	Age:	Temperament (1-10):

Veterinarian:	HOOF ANGLES			HOOF LENGTHS		
		Left	Right		Left	Right
Trainer:	Front			Front		
	Back			Back		
Health Concerns:	Supplements:			Shoe Size:		
				Shoe Type:		
				Shoe Pads:		
Therapeutic Treatments:	Special Requirements:			Dates Due:		
Notes (Problems, Consultations, Changes, etc.):				Stable Name / Address:		

CLIENT INFORMATION	Name:		
	Address:		
	Phone:		Email:

HORSE INFORMATION	Name:		Breed:
	Gender:		Primary Use:
	Age:		Temperament (1-10):

Veterinarian:	HOOF ANGLES			HOOF LENGTHS		
		Left	Right		Left	Right
Trainer:	Front			Front		
	Back			Back		

Health Concerns:	Supplements:	Shoe Size:
		Shoe Type:
		Shoe Pads:
Therapeutic Treatments:	Special Requirements:	Dates Due:

| Notes (Problems, Consultations, Changes, etc.): | Stable Name / Address: |

CLIENT INFORMATION	Name:		
	Address:		
	Phone:		Email:

HORSE INFORMATION	Name:		Breed:
	Gender:		Primary Use:
	Age:		Temperament (1-10):

Veterinarian:	HOOF ANGLES			HOOF LENGTHS		
		Left	Right		Left	Right
Trainer:	Front			Front		
	Back			Back		

Health Concerns:	Supplements:	Shoe Size:
		Shoe Type:
		Shoe Pads:
Therapeutic Treatments:	Special Requirements:	Dates Due:

| Notes (Problems, Consultations, Changes, etc.): | Stable Name / Address: |

CLIENT INFORMATION	Name:		
	Address:		
	Phone:		Email:

HORSE INFORMATION	Name:		Breed:
	Gender:		Primary Use:
	Age:		Temperament (1-10):

Veterinarian:	HOOF ANGLES			HOOF LENGTHS		
		Left	Right		Left	Right
Trainer:	Front			Front		
	Back			Back		

Health Concerns:	Supplements:	Shoe Size:
		Shoe Type:
		Shoe Pads:
Therapeutic Treatments:	Special Requirements:	Dates Due:
Notes (Problems, Consultations, Changes, etc.):		Stable Name / Address:

CLIENT INFORMATION	Name:		
	Address:		
	Phone:		Email:

HORSE INFORMATION	Name:		Breed:
	Gender:		Primary Use:
	Age:		Temperament (1-10):

Veterinarian:	HOOF ANGLES			HOOF LENGTHS		
		Left	Right		Left	Right
Trainer:	Front			Front		
	Back			Back		

Health Concerns:	Supplements:	Shoe Size:
		Shoe Type:
		Shoe Pads:
Therapeutic Treatments:	Special Requirements:	Dates Due:
Notes (Problems, Consultations, Changes, etc.):		Stable Name / Address:

CLIENT INFORMATION	Name:						
	Address:						
	Phone:			Email:			
HORSE INFORMATION	Name:			Breed:			
	Gender:			Primary Use:			
	Age:			Temperament (1-10):			

Veterinarian:	HOOF ANGLES			HOOF LENGTHS		
		Left	Right		Left	Right
Trainer:	Front			Front		
	Back			Back		

Health Concerns:	Supplements:	Shoe Size:
		Shoe Type:
		Shoe Pads:
Therapeutic Treatments:	Special Requirements:	Dates Due:
Notes (Problems, Consultations, Changes, etc.):		Stable Name / Address:

CLIENT INFORMATION	Name:						
	Address:						
	Phone:			Email:			
HORSE INFORMATION	Name:			Breed:			
	Gender:			Primary Use:			
	Age:			Temperament (1-10):			

Veterinarian:	HOOF ANGLES			HOOF LENGTHS		
		Left	Right		Left	Right
Trainer:	Front			Front		
	Back			Back		

Health Concerns:	Supplements:	Shoe Size:
		Shoe Type:
		Shoe Pads:
Therapeutic Treatments:	Special Requirements:	Dates Due:
Notes (Problems, Consultations, Changes, etc.):		Stable Name / Address:

CLIENT INFORMATION	Name:		
	Address:		
	Phone:		Email:

HORSE INFORMATION	Name:		Breed:
	Gender:		Primary Use:
	Age:		Temperament (1-10):

Veterinarian:	HOOF ANGLES			HOOF LENGTHS		
		Left	Right		Left	Right
Trainer:	Front			Front		
	Back			Back		

Health Concerns:	Supplements:	Shoe Size:
		Shoe Type:
		Shoe Pads:
Therapeutic Treatments:	Special Requirements:	Dates Due:

| Notes (Problems, Consultations, Changes, etc.): | Stable Name / Address: |

CLIENT INFORMATION	Name:		
	Address:		
	Phone:		Email:

HORSE INFORMATION	Name:		Breed:
	Gender:		Primary Use:
	Age:		Temperament (1-10):

Veterinarian:	HOOF ANGLES			HOOF LENGTHS		
		Left	Right		Left	Right
Trainer:	Front			Front		
	Back			Back		

Health Concerns:	Supplements:	Shoe Size:
		Shoe Type:
		Shoe Pads:
Therapeutic Treatments:	Special Requirements:	Dates Due:

| Notes (Problems, Consultations, Changes, etc.): | Stable Name / Address: |

CLIENT INFORMATION	Name:	
	Address:	
	Phone:	Email:

HORSE INFORMATION	Name:	Breed:
	Gender:	Primary Use:
	Age:	Temperament (1-10):

Veterinarian:	HOOF ANGLES			HOOF LENGTHS		
		Left	Right		Left	Right
Trainer:	Front			Front		
	Back			Back		
Health Concerns:	Supplements:			Shoe Size:		
				Shoe Type:		
				Shoe Pads:		
Therapeutic Treatments:	Special Requirements:			Dates Due:		
Notes (Problems, Consultations, Changes, etc.):				Stable Name / Address:		

CLIENT INFORMATION	Name:	
	Address:	
	Phone:	Email:

HORSE INFORMATION	Name:	Breed:
	Gender:	Primary Use:
	Age:	Temperament (1-10):

Veterinarian:	HOOF ANGLES			HOOF LENGTHS		
		Left	Right		Left	Right
Trainer:	Front			Front		
	Back			Back		
Health Concerns:	Supplements:			Shoe Size:		
				Shoe Type:		
				Shoe Pads:		
Therapeutic Treatments:	Special Requirements:			Dates Due:		
Notes (Problems, Consultations, Changes, etc.):				Stable Name / Address:		

CLIENT INFORMATION	Name:						
	Address:						
	Phone:				Email:		
HORSE INFORMATION	Name:				Breed:		
	Gender:				Primary Use:		
	Age:				Temperament (1-10):		

Veterinarian:	HOOF ANGLES			HOOF LENGTHS		
		Left	Right		Left	Right
Trainer:	Front			Front		
	Back			Back		

Health Concerns:	Supplements:	Shoe Size:
		Shoe Type:
		Shoe Pads:
Therapeutic Treatments:	Special Requirements:	Dates Due:
Notes (Problems, Consultations, Changes, etc.):		Stable Name / Address:

CLIENT INFORMATION	Name:						
	Address:						
	Phone:				Email:		
HORSE INFORMATION	Name:				Breed:		
	Gender:				Primary Use:		
	Age:				Temperament (1-10):		

Veterinarian:	HOOF ANGLES			HOOF LENGTHS		
		Left	Right		Left	Right
Trainer:	Front			Front		
	Back			Back		

Health Concerns:	Supplements:	Shoe Size:
		Shoe Type:
		Shoe Pads:
Therapeutic Treatments:	Special Requirements:	Dates Due:
Notes (Problems, Consultations, Changes, etc.):		Stable Name / Address:

CLIENT INFORMATION	Name:		
	Address:		
	Phone:		Email:

HORSE INFORMATION	Name:		Breed:
	Gender:		Primary Use:
	Age:		Temperament (1-10):

Veterinarian:	HOOF ANGLES			HOOF LENGTHS		
		Left	Right		Left	Right
Trainer:	Front			Front		
	Back			Back		
Health Concerns:	Supplements:			Shoe Size:		
				Shoe Type:		
				Shoe Pads:		
Therapeutic Treatments:	Special Requirements:			Dates Due:		
Notes (Problems, Consultations, Changes, etc.):				Stable Name / Address:		

CLIENT INFORMATION	Name:		
	Address:		
	Phone:		Email:

HORSE INFORMATION	Name:		Breed:
	Gender:		Primary Use:
	Age:		Temperament (1-10):

Veterinarian:	HOOF ANGLES			HOOF LENGTHS		
		Left	Right		Left	Right
Trainer:	Front			Front		
	Back			Back		
Health Concerns:	Supplements:			Shoe Size:		
				Shoe Type:		
				Shoe Pads:		
Therapeutic Treatments:	Special Requirements:			Dates Due:		
Notes (Problems, Consultations, Changes, etc.):				Stable Name / Address:		

CLIENT INFORMATION	Name:					
	Address:					
	Phone:			Email:		

HORSE INFORMATION	Name:			Breed:		
	Gender:			Primary Use:		
	Age:			Temperament (1-10):		

Veterinarian:	HOOF ANGLES			HOOF LENGTHS		
		Left	Right		Left	Right
Trainer:	Front			Front		
	Back			Back		
Health Concerns:	Supplements:			Shoe Size:		
				Shoe Type:		
				Shoe Pads:		
Therapeutic Treatments:	Special Requirements:			Dates Due:		
Notes (Problems, Consultations, Changes, etc.):				Stable Name / Address:		

CLIENT INFORMATION	Name:					
	Address:					
	Phone:			Email:		

HORSE INFORMATION	Name:			Breed:		
	Gender:			Primary Use:		
	Age:			Temperament (1-10):		

Veterinarian:	HOOF ANGLES			HOOF LENGTHS		
		Left	Right		Left	Right
Trainer:	Front			Front		
	Back			Back		
Health Concerns:	Supplements:			Shoe Size:		
				Shoe Type:		
				Shoe Pads:		
Therapeutic Treatments:	Special Requirements:			Dates Due:		
Notes (Problems, Consultations, Changes, etc.):				Stable Name / Address:		

CLIENT INFORMATION	Name:		
	Address:		
	Phone:		Email:

HORSE INFORMATION	Name:		Breed:
	Gender:		Primary Use:
	Age:		Temperament (1-10):

Veterinarian:	HOOF ANGLES			HOOF LENGTHS		
		Left	Right		Left	Right
Trainer:	Front			Front		
	Back			Back		
Health Concerns:	Supplements:			Shoe Size:		
				Shoe Type:		
				Shoe Pads:		
Therapeutic Treatments:	Special Requirements:			Dates Due:		
Notes (Problems, Consultations, Changes, etc.):				Stable Name / Address:		

CLIENT INFORMATION	Name:		
	Address:		
	Phone:		Email:

HORSE INFORMATION	Name:		Breed:
	Gender:		Primary Use:
	Age:		Temperament (1-10):

Veterinarian:	HOOF ANGLES			HOOF LENGTHS		
		Left	Right		Left	Right
Trainer:	Front			Front		
	Back			Back		
Health Concerns:	Supplements:			Shoe Size:		
				Shoe Type:		
				Shoe Pads:		
Therapeutic Treatments:	Special Requirements:			Dates Due:		
Notes (Problems, Consultations, Changes, etc.):				Stable Name / Address:		

CLIENT INFORMATION	Name:						
	Address:						
	Phone:			Email:			
HORSE INFORMATION	Name:			Breed:			
	Gender:			Primary Use:			
	Age:			Temperament (1-10):			

Veterinarian:	HOOF ANGLES			HOOF LENGTHS		
		Left	Right		Left	Right
Trainer:	Front			Front		
	Back			Back		
Health Concerns:	Supplements:			Shoe Size:		
				Shoe Type:		
				Shoe Pads:		
Therapeutic Treatments:	Special Requirements:			Dates Due:		
Notes (Problems, Consultations, Changes, etc.):				Stable Name / Address:		

CLIENT INFORMATION	Name:						
	Address:						
	Phone:			Email:			
HORSE INFORMATION	Name:			Breed:			
	Gender:			Primary Use:			
	Age:			Temperament (1-10):			

Veterinarian:	HOOF ANGLES			HOOF LENGTHS		
		Left	Right		Left	Right
Trainer:	Front			Front		
	Back			Back		
Health Concerns:	Supplements:			Shoe Size:		
				Shoe Type:		
				Shoe Pads:		
Therapeutic Treatments:	Special Requirements:			Dates Due:		
Notes (Problems, Consultations, Changes, etc.):				Stable Name / Address:		

CLIENT INFORMATION	Name:	
	Address:	
	Phone:	Email:

HORSE INFORMATION	Name:	Breed:
	Gender:	Primary Use:
	Age:	Temperament (1-10):

Veterinarian:	HOOF ANGLES			HOOF LENGTHS		
		Left	Right		Left	Right
Trainer:	Front			Front		
	Back			Back		
Health Concerns:	Supplements:			Shoe Size:		
				Shoe Type:		
				Shoe Pads:		
Therapeutic Treatments:	Special Requirements:			Dates Due:		
Notes (Problems, Consultations, Changes, etc.):				Stable Name / Address:		

CLIENT INFORMATION	Name:	
	Address:	
	Phone:	Email:

HORSE INFORMATION	Name:	Breed:
	Gender:	Primary Use:
	Age:	Temperament (1-10):

Veterinarian:	HOOF ANGLES			HOOF LENGTHS		
		Left	Right		Left	Right
Trainer:	Front			Front		
	Back			Back		
Health Concerns:	Supplements:			Shoe Size:		
				Shoe Type:		
				Shoe Pads:		
Therapeutic Treatments:	Special Requirements:			Dates Due:		
Notes (Problems, Consultations, Changes, etc.):				Stable Name / Address:		

CLIENT INFORMATION	Name:		
	Address:		
	Phone:		Email:

HORSE INFORMATION	Name:		Breed:
	Gender:		Primary Use:
	Age:		Temperament (1-10):

Veterinarian:	HOOF ANGLES			HOOF LENGTHS		
		Left	Right		Left	Right
Trainer:	Front			Front		
	Back			Back		

Health Concerns:	Supplements:	Shoe Size:
		Shoe Type:
		Shoe Pads:
Therapeutic Treatments:	Special Requirements:	Dates Due:
Notes (Problems, Consultations, Changes, etc.):		Stable Name / Address:

CLIENT INFORMATION	Name:		
	Address:		
	Phone:		Email:

HORSE INFORMATION	Name:		Breed:
	Gender:		Primary Use:
	Age:		Temperament (1-10):

Veterinarian:	HOOF ANGLES			HOOF LENGTHS		
		Left	Right		Left	Right
Trainer:	Front			Front		
	Back			Back		

Health Concerns:	Supplements:	Shoe Size:
		Shoe Type:
		Shoe Pads:
Therapeutic Treatments:	Special Requirements:	Dates Due:
Notes (Problems, Consultations, Changes, etc.):		Stable Name / Address:

CLIENT INFORMATION	Name:	
	Address:	
	Phone:	Email:

HORSE INFORMATION	Name:	Breed:
	Gender:	Primary Use:
	Age:	Temperament (1-10):

Veterinarian:	HOOF ANGLES			HOOF LENGTHS		
		Left	Right		Left	Right
Trainer:	Front			Front		
	Back			Back		
Health Concerns:	Supplements:			Shoe Size:		
				Shoe Type:		
				Shoe Pads:		
Therapeutic Treatments:	Special Requirements:			Dates Due:		
Notes (Problems, Consultations, Changes, etc.):				Stable Name / Address:		

CLIENT INFORMATION	Name:	
	Address:	
	Phone:	Email:

HORSE INFORMATION	Name:	Breed:
	Gender:	Primary Use:
	Age:	Temperament (1-10):

Veterinarian:	HOOF ANGLES			HOOF LENGTHS		
		Left	Right		Left	Right
Trainer:	Front			Front		
	Back			Back		
Health Concerns:	Supplements:			Shoe Size:		
				Shoe Type:		
				Shoe Pads:		
Therapeutic Treatments:	Special Requirements:			Dates Due:		
Notes (Problems, Consultations, Changes, etc.):				Stable Name / Address:		

CLIENT INFORMATION	Name:			
	Address:			
	Phone:		Email:	

HORSE INFORMATION	Name:		Breed:	
	Gender:		Primary Use:	
	Age:		Temperament (1-10):	

Veterinarian:	HOOF ANGLES			HOOF LENGTHS		
		Left	Right		Left	Right
Trainer:	Front			Front		
	Back			Back		

Health Concerns:	Supplements:	Shoe Size:
		Shoe Type:
		Shoe Pads:
Therapeutic Treatments:	Special Requirements:	Dates Due:

| Notes (Problems, Consultations, Changes, etc.): | Stable Name / Address: |

CLIENT INFORMATION	Name:			
	Address:			
	Phone:		Email:	

HORSE INFORMATION	Name:		Breed:	
	Gender:		Primary Use:	
	Age:		Temperament (1-10):	

Veterinarian:	HOOF ANGLES			HOOF LENGTHS		
		Left	Right		Left	Right
Trainer:	Front			Front		
	Back			Back		

Health Concerns:	Supplements:	Shoe Size:
		Shoe Type:
		Shoe Pads:
Therapeutic Treatments:	Special Requirements:	Dates Due:

| Notes (Problems, Consultations, Changes, etc.): | Stable Name / Address: |

CLIENT INFORMATION	Name:						
	Address:						
	Phone:			Email:			

HORSE INFORMATION	Name:			Breed:			
	Gender:			Primary Use:			
	Age:			Temperament (1-10):			

Veterinarian:	HOOF ANGLES			HOOF LENGTHS			
		Left	Right			Left	Right
Trainer:	Front				Front		
	Back				Back		

Health Concerns:	Supplements:	Shoe Size:
		Shoe Type:
		Shoe Pads:
Therapeutic Treatments:	Special Requirements:	Dates Due:

Notes (Problems, Consultations, Changes, etc.):	Stable Name / Address:

CLIENT INFORMATION	Name:						
	Address:						
	Phone:			Email:			

HORSE INFORMATION	Name:			Breed:			
	Gender:			Primary Use:			
	Age:			Temperament (1-10):			

Veterinarian:	HOOF ANGLES			HOOF LENGTHS			
		Left	Right			Left	Right
Trainer:	Front				Front		
	Back				Back		

Health Concerns:	Supplements:	Shoe Size:
		Shoe Type:
		Shoe Pads:
Therapeutic Treatments:	Special Requirements:	Dates Due:

Notes (Problems, Consultations, Changes, etc.):	Stable Name / Address:

CLIENT INFORMATION	Name:				
	Address:				
	Phone:			Email:	

HORSE INFORMATION	Name:			Breed:	
	Gender:			Primary Use:	
	Age:			Temperament (1-10):	

Veterinarian:	HOOF ANGLES			HOOF LENGTHS		
		Left	Right		Left	Right
Trainer:	Front			Front		
	Back			Back		

Health Concerns:	Supplements:	Shoe Size:
		Shoe Type:
		Shoe Pads:
Therapeutic Treatments:	Special Requirements:	Dates Due:

| Notes (Problems, Consultations, Changes, etc.): | Stable Name / Address: |

CLIENT INFORMATION	Name:				
	Address:				
	Phone:			Email:	

HORSE INFORMATION	Name:			Breed:	
	Gender:			Primary Use:	
	Age:			Temperament (1-10):	

Veterinarian:	HOOF ANGLES			HOOF LENGTHS		
		Left	Right		Left	Right
Trainer:	Front			Front		
	Back			Back		

Health Concerns:	Supplements:	Shoe Size:
		Shoe Type:
		Shoe Pads:
Therapeutic Treatments:	Special Requirements:	Dates Due:

| Notes (Problems, Consultations, Changes, etc.): | Stable Name / Address: |

CLIENT INFORMATION	Name:						
	Address:						
	Phone:			Email:			
HORSE INFORMATION	Name:			Breed:			
	Gender:			Primary Use:			
	Age:			Temperament (1-10):			

Veterinarian:	HOOF ANGLES			HOOF LENGTHS		
		Left	Right		Left	Right
Trainer:	Front			Front		
	Back			Back		
Health Concerns:	Supplements:			Shoe Size:		
				Shoe Type:		
				Shoe Pads:		
Therapeutic Treatments:	Special Requirements:			Dates Due:		
Notes (Problems, Consultations, Changes, etc.):				Stable Name / Address:		

CLIENT INFORMATION	Name:						
	Address:						
	Phone:			Email:			
HORSE INFORMATION	Name:			Breed:			
	Gender:			Primary Use:			
	Age:			Temperament (1-10):			

Veterinarian:	HOOF ANGLES			HOOF LENGTHS		
		Left	Right		Left	Right
Trainer:	Front			Front		
	Back			Back		
Health Concerns:	Supplements:			Shoe Size:		
				Shoe Type:		
				Shoe Pads:		
Therapeutic Treatments:	Special Requirements:			Dates Due:		
Notes (Problems, Consultations, Changes, etc.):				Stable Name / Address:		

CLIENT INFORMATION	Name:						
	Address:						
	Phone:			Email:			
HORSE INFORMATION	Name:			Breed:			
	Gender:			Primary Use:			
	Age:			Temperament (1-10):			
Veterinarian:	HOOF ANGLES			HOOF LENGTHS			
		Left	Right			Left	Right
Trainer:	Front				Front		
	Back				Back		
Health Concerns:	Supplements:			Shoe Size:			
				Shoe Type:			
				Shoe Pads:			
Therapeutic Treatments:	Special Requirements:			Dates Due:			
Notes (Problems, Consultations, Changes, etc.):				Stable Name / Address:			

CLIENT INFORMATION	Name:						
	Address:						
	Phone:			Email:			
HORSE INFORMATION	Name:			Breed:			
	Gender:			Primary Use:			
	Age:			Temperament (1-10):			
Veterinarian:	HOOF ANGLES			HOOF LENGTHS			
		Left	Right			Left	Right
Trainer:	Front				Front		
	Back				Back		
Health Concerns:	Supplements:			Shoe Size:			
				Shoe Type:			
				Shoe Pads:			
Therapeutic Treatments:	Special Requirements:			Dates Due:			
Notes (Problems, Consultations, Changes, etc.):				Stable Name / Address:			

CLIENT INFORMATION	Name:		
	Address:		
	Phone:		Email:

HORSE INFORMATION	Name:		Breed:
	Gender:		Primary Use:
	Age:		Temperament (1-10):

Veterinarian:	HOOF ANGLES			HOOF LENGTHS		
		Left	Right		Left	Right
Trainer:	Front			Front		
	Back			Back		

Health Concerns:	Supplements:	Shoe Size:
		Shoe Type:
		Shoe Pads:
Therapeutic Treatments:	Special Requirements:	Dates Due:

| Notes (Problems, Consultations, Changes, etc.): | Stable Name / Address: |

CLIENT INFORMATION	Name:		
	Address:		
	Phone:		Email:

HORSE INFORMATION	Name:		Breed:
	Gender:		Primary Use:
	Age:		Temperament (1-10):

Veterinarian:	HOOF ANGLES			HOOF LENGTHS		
		Left	Right		Left	Right
Trainer:	Front			Front		
	Back			Back		

Health Concerns:	Supplements:	Shoe Size:
		Shoe Type:
		Shoe Pads:
Therapeutic Treatments:	Special Requirements:	Dates Due:

| Notes (Problems, Consultations, Changes, etc.): | Stable Name / Address: |

CLIENT INFORMATION	Name:			
	Address:			
	Phone:		Email:	

HORSE INFORMATION	Name:		Breed:	
	Gender:		Primary Use:	
	Age:		Temperament (1-10):	

Veterinarian:	HOOF ANGLES			HOOF LENGTHS		
		Left	Right		Left	Right
Trainer:	Front			Front		
	Back			Back		

Health Concerns:	Supplements:	Shoe Size:
		Shoe Type:
		Shoe Pads:
Therapeutic Treatments:	Special Requirements:	Dates Due:
Notes (Problems, Consultations, Changes, etc.):		Stable Name / Address:

CLIENT INFORMATION	Name:			
	Address:			
	Phone:		Email:	

HORSE INFORMATION	Name:		Breed:	
	Gender:		Primary Use:	
	Age:		Temperament (1-10):	

Veterinarian:	HOOF ANGLES			HOOF LENGTHS		
		Left	Right		Left	Right
Trainer:	Front			Front		
	Back			Back		

Health Concerns:	Supplements:	Shoe Size:
		Shoe Type:
		Shoe Pads:
Therapeutic Treatments:	Special Requirements:	Dates Due:
Notes (Problems, Consultations, Changes, etc.):		Stable Name / Address:

CLIENT INFORMATION	Name:						
	Address:						
	Phone:				Email:		
HORSE INFORMATION	Name:				Breed:		
	Gender:				Primary Use:		
	Age:				Temperament (1-10):		

Veterinarian:	HOOF ANGLES			HOOF LENGTHS		
		Left	Right		Left	Right
Trainer:	Front			Front		
	Back			Back		

Health Concerns:	Supplements:	Shoe Size:
		Shoe Type:
		Shoe Pads:
Therapeutic Treatments:	Special Requirements:	Dates Due:
Notes (Problems, Consultations, Changes, etc.):		Stable Name / Address:

CLIENT INFORMATION	Name:						
	Address:						
	Phone:				Email:		
HORSE INFORMATION	Name:				Breed:		
	Gender:				Primary Use:		
	Age:				Temperament (1-10):		

Veterinarian:	HOOF ANGLES			HOOF LENGTHS		
		Left	Right		Left	Right
Trainer:	Front			Front		
	Back			Back		

Health Concerns:	Supplements:	Shoe Size:
		Shoe Type:
		Shoe Pads:
Therapeutic Treatments:	Special Requirements:	Dates Due:
Notes (Problems, Consultations, Changes, etc.):		Stable Name / Address:

CLIENT INFORMATION	Name:						
	Address:						
	Phone:				Email:		
HORSE INFORMATION	Name:				Breed:		
	Gender:				Primary Use:		
	Age:				Temperament (1-10):		

Veterinarian:	HOOF ANGLES			HOOF LENGTHS		
		Left	Right		Left	Right
Trainer:	Front			Front		
	Back			Back		

Health Concerns:	Supplements:	Shoe Size:
		Shoe Type:
		Shoe Pads:
Therapeutic Treatments:	Special Requirements:	Dates Due:
Notes (Problems, Consultations, Changes, etc.):		Stable Name / Address:

CLIENT INFORMATION	Name:						
	Address:						
	Phone:				Email:		
HORSE INFORMATION	Name:				Breed:		
	Gender:				Primary Use:		
	Age:				Temperament (1-10):		

Veterinarian:	HOOF ANGLES			HOOF LENGTHS		
		Left	Right		Left	Right
Trainer:	Front			Front		
	Back			Back		

Health Concerns:	Supplements:	Shoe Size:
		Shoe Type:
		Shoe Pads:
Therapeutic Treatments:	Special Requirements:	Dates Due:
Notes (Problems, Consultations, Changes, etc.):		Stable Name / Address:

CLIENT INFORMATION	Name:					
	Address:					
	Phone:			Email:		

HORSE INFORMATION	Name:			Breed:		
	Gender:			Primary Use:		
	Age:			Temperament (1-10):		

Veterinarian:	HOOF ANGLES			HOOF LENGTHS		
		Left	Right		Left	Right
Trainer:	Front			Front		
	Back			Back		

Health Concerns:	Supplements:	Shoe Size:
		Shoe Type:
		Shoe Pads:
Therapeutic Treatments:	Special Requirements:	Dates Due:
Notes (Problems, Consultations, Changes, etc.):		Stable Name / Address:

CLIENT INFORMATION	Name:					
	Address:					
	Phone:			Email:		

HORSE INFORMATION	Name:			Breed:		
	Gender:			Primary Use:		
	Age:			Temperament (1-10):		

Veterinarian:	HOOF ANGLES			HOOF LENGTHS		
		Left	Right		Left	Right
Trainer:	Front			Front		
	Back			Back		

Health Concerns:	Supplements:	Shoe Size:
		Shoe Type:
		Shoe Pads:
Therapeutic Treatments:	Special Requirements:	Dates Due:
Notes (Problems, Consultations, Changes, etc.):		Stable Name / Address:

CLIENT INFORMATION	Name:						
	Address:						
	Phone:			Email:			
HORSE INFORMATION	Name:			Breed:			
	Gender:			Primary Use:			
	Age:			Temperament (1-10):			

Veterinarian:	HOOF ANGLES			HOOF LENGTHS		
		Left	Right		Left	Right
Trainer:	Front			Front		
	Back			Back		

Health Concerns:	Supplements:	Shoe Size:
		Shoe Type:
		Shoe Pads:
Therapeutic Treatments:	Special Requirements:	Dates Due:
Notes (Problems, Consultations, Changes, etc.):		Stable Name / Address:

CLIENT INFORMATION	Name:						
	Address:						
	Phone:			Email:			
HORSE INFORMATION	Name:			Breed:			
	Gender:			Primary Use:			
	Age:			Temperament (1-10):			

Veterinarian:	HOOF ANGLES			HOOF LENGTHS		
		Left	Right		Left	Right
Trainer:	Front			Front		
	Back			Back		

Health Concerns:	Supplements:	Shoe Size:
		Shoe Type:
		Shoe Pads:
Therapeutic Treatments:	Special Requirements:	Dates Due:
Notes (Problems, Consultations, Changes, etc.):		Stable Name / Address:

CLIENT INFORMATION	Name:						
	Address:						
	Phone:			Email:			
HORSE INFORMATION	Name:			Breed:			
	Gender:			Primary Use:			
	Age:			Temperament (1-10):			

Veterinarian:	HOOF ANGLES			HOOF LENGTHS		
		Left	Right		Left	Right
Trainer:	Front			Front		
	Back			Back		

Health Concerns:	Supplements:	Shoe Size:
		Shoe Type:
		Shoe Pads:
Therapeutic Treatments:	Special Requirements:	Dates Due:
Notes (Problems, Consultations, Changes, etc.):		Stable Name / Address:

CLIENT INFORMATION	Name:						
	Address:						
	Phone:			Email:			
HORSE INFORMATION	Name:			Breed:			
	Gender:			Primary Use:			
	Age:			Temperament (1-10):			

Veterinarian:	HOOF ANGLES			HOOF LENGTHS		
		Left	Right		Left	Right
Trainer:	Front			Front		
	Back			Back		

Health Concerns:	Supplements:	Shoe Size:
		Shoe Type:
		Shoe Pads:
Therapeutic Treatments:	Special Requirements:	Dates Due:
Notes (Problems, Consultations, Changes, etc.):		Stable Name / Address:

CLIENT INFORMATION	Name:	
	Address:	
	Phone:	Email:

HORSE INFORMATION	Name:	Breed:
	Gender:	Primary Use:
	Age:	Temperament (1-10):

Veterinarian:	HOOF ANGLES			HOOF LENGTHS		
		Left	Right		Left	Right
Trainer:	Front			Front		
	Back			Back		
Health Concerns:	Supplements:			Shoe Size:		
				Shoe Type:		
				Shoe Pads:		
Therapeutic Treatments:	Special Requirements:			Dates Due:		
Notes (Problems, Consultations, Changes, etc.):				Stable Name / Address:		

CLIENT INFORMATION	Name:	
	Address:	
	Phone:	Email:

HORSE INFORMATION	Name:	Breed:
	Gender:	Primary Use:
	Age:	Temperament (1-10):

Veterinarian:	HOOF ANGLES			HOOF LENGTHS		
		Left	Right		Left	Right
Trainer:	Front			Front		
	Back			Back		
Health Concerns:	Supplements:			Shoe Size:		
				Shoe Type:		
				Shoe Pads:		
Therapeutic Treatments:	Special Requirements:			Dates Due:		
Notes (Problems, Consultations, Changes, etc.):				Stable Name / Address:		

CLIENT INFORMATION	Name:					
	Address:					
	Phone:			Email:		

HORSE INFORMATION	Name:			Breed:		
	Gender:			Primary Use:		
	Age:			Temperament (1-10):		

Veterinarian:	HOOF ANGLES			HOOF LENGTHS		
		Left	Right		Left	Right
Trainer:	Front			Front		
	Back			Back		
Health Concerns:	Supplements:			Shoe Size:		
				Shoe Type:		
				Shoe Pads:		
Therapeutic Treatments:	Special Requirements:			Dates Due:		
Notes (Problems, Consultations, Changes, etc.):				Stable Name / Address:		

CLIENT INFORMATION	Name:					
	Address:					
	Phone:			Email:		

HORSE INFORMATION	Name:			Breed:		
	Gender:			Primary Use:		
	Age:			Temperament (1-10):		

Veterinarian:	HOOF ANGLES			HOOF LENGTHS		
		Left	Right		Left	Right
Trainer:	Front			Front		
	Back			Back		
Health Concerns:	Supplements:			Shoe Size:		
				Shoe Type:		
				Shoe Pads:		
Therapeutic Treatments:	Special Requirements:			Dates Due:		
Notes (Problems, Consultations, Changes, etc.):				Stable Name / Address:		

CLIENT INFORMATION	Name:						
	Address:						
	Phone:			Email:			
HORSE INFORMATION	Name:			Breed:			
	Gender:			Primary Use:			
	Age:			Temperament (1-10):			
Veterinarian:	HOOF ANGLES			HOOF LENGTHS			
		Left	Right			Left	Right
Trainer:	Front				Front		
	Back				Back		
Health Concerns:	Supplements:			Shoe Size:			
				Shoe Type:			
				Shoe Pads:			
Therapeutic Treatments:	Special Requirements:			Dates Due:			
Notes (Problems, Consultations, Changes, etc.):				Stable Name / Address:			

CLIENT INFORMATION	Name:						
	Address:						
	Phone:			Email:			
HORSE INFORMATION	Name:			Breed:			
	Gender:			Primary Use:			
	Age:			Temperament (1-10):			
Veterinarian:	HOOF ANGLES			HOOF LENGTHS			
		Left	Right			Left	Right
Trainer:	Front				Front		
	Back				Back		
Health Concerns:	Supplements:			Shoe Size:			
				Shoe Type:			
				Shoe Pads:			
Therapeutic Treatments:	Special Requirements:			Dates Due:			
Notes (Problems, Consultations, Changes, etc.):				Stable Name / Address:			

CLIENT INFORMATION	Name:						
	Address:						
	Phone:			Email:			
HORSE INFORMATION	Name:			Breed:			
	Gender:			Primary Use:			
	Age:			Temperament (1-10):			

Veterinarian:	HOOF ANGLES			HOOF LENGTHS		
		Left	Right		Left	Right
Trainer:	Front			Front		
	Back			Back		
Health Concerns:	Supplements:			Shoe Size:		
				Shoe Type:		
				Shoe Pads:		
Therapeutic Treatments:	Special Requirements:			Dates Due:		
Notes (Problems, Consultations, Changes, etc.):				Stable Name / Address:		

CLIENT INFORMATION	Name:						
	Address:						
	Phone:			Email:			
HORSE INFORMATION	Name:			Breed:			
	Gender:			Primary Use:			
	Age:			Temperament (1-10):			

Veterinarian:	HOOF ANGLES			HOOF LENGTHS		
		Left	Right		Left	Right
Trainer:	Front			Front		
	Back			Back		
Health Concerns:	Supplements:			Shoe Size:		
				Shoe Type:		
				Shoe Pads:		
Therapeutic Treatments:	Special Requirements:			Dates Due:		
Notes (Problems, Consultations, Changes, etc.):				Stable Name / Address:		

CLIENT INFORMATION	Name:	
	Address:	
	Phone:	Email:

HORSE INFORMATION	Name:	Breed:
	Gender:	Primary Use:
	Age:	Temperament (1-10):

Veterinarian:

HOOF ANGLES			HOOF LENGTHS		
	Left	Right		Left	Right
Front			Front		
Back			Back		

Trainer:

Health Concerns: | **Supplements:** | Shoe Size:

Shoe Type:

Shoe Pads:

Therapeutic Treatments: | **Special Requirements:** | **Dates Due:**

Notes (Problems, Consultations, Changes, etc.): | **Stable Name / Address:**

CLIENT INFORMATION	Name:	
	Address:	
	Phone:	Email:

HORSE INFORMATION	Name:	Breed:
	Gender:	Primary Use:
	Age:	Temperament (1-10):

Veterinarian:

HOOF ANGLES			HOOF LENGTHS		
	Left	Right		Left	Right
Front			Front		
Back			Back		

Trainer:

Health Concerns: | **Supplements:** | Shoe Size:

Shoe Type:

Shoe Pads:

Therapeutic Treatments: | **Special Requirements:** | **Dates Due:**

Notes (Problems, Consultations, Changes, etc.): | **Stable Name / Address:**

CLIENT INFORMATION	Name:						
	Address:						
	Phone:				Email:		
HORSE INFORMATION	Name:				Breed:		
	Gender:				Primary Use:		
	Age:				Temperament (1-10):		

Veterinarian:	HOOF ANGLES			HOOF LENGTHS		
		Left	Right		Left	Right
Trainer:	Front			Front		
	Back			Back		

Health Concerns:	Supplements:	Shoe Size:
		Shoe Type:
		Shoe Pads:
Therapeutic Treatments:	Special Requirements:	Dates Due:
Notes (Problems, Consultations, Changes, etc.):		Stable Name / Address:

CLIENT INFORMATION	Name:						
	Address:						
	Phone:				Email:		
HORSE INFORMATION	Name:				Breed:		
	Gender:				Primary Use:		
	Age:				Temperament (1-10):		

Veterinarian:	HOOF ANGLES			HOOF LENGTHS		
		Left	Right		Left	Right
Trainer:	Front			Front		
	Back			Back		

Health Concerns:	Supplements:	Shoe Size:
		Shoe Type:
		Shoe Pads:
Therapeutic Treatments:	Special Requirements:	Dates Due:
Notes (Problems, Consultations, Changes, etc.):		Stable Name / Address:

CLIENT INFORMATION	Name:						
	Address:						
	Phone:			Email:			
HORSE INFORMATION	Name:			Breed:			
	Gender:			Primary Use:			
	Age:			Temperament (1-10):			

Veterinarian:	HOOF ANGLES			HOOF LENGTHS		
		Left	Right		Left	Right
Trainer:	Front			Front		
	Back			Back		

Health Concerns:	Supplements:	Shoe Size:
		Shoe Type:
		Shoe Pads:
Therapeutic Treatments:	Special Requirements:	Dates Due:
Notes (Problems, Consultations, Changes, etc.):		Stable Name / Address:

CLIENT INFORMATION	Name:						
	Address:						
	Phone:			Email:			
HORSE INFORMATION	Name:			Breed:			
	Gender:			Primary Use:			
	Age:			Temperament (1-10):			

Veterinarian:	HOOF ANGLES			HOOF LENGTHS		
		Left	Right		Left	Right
Trainer:	Front			Front		
	Back			Back		

Health Concerns:	Supplements:	Shoe Size:
		Shoe Type:
		Shoe Pads:
Therapeutic Treatments:	Special Requirements:	Dates Due:
Notes (Problems, Consultations, Changes, etc.):		Stable Name / Address:

CLIENT INFORMATION	Name:		
	Address:		
	Phone:		Email:

HORSE INFORMATION	Name:		Breed:
	Gender:		Primary Use:
	Age:		Temperament (1-10):

Veterinarian:	HOOF ANGLES			HOOF LENGTHS		
		Left	Right		Left	Right
Trainer:	Front			Front		
	Back			Back		
Health Concerns:	Supplements:			Shoe Size:		
				Shoe Type:		
				Shoe Pads:		
Therapeutic Treatments:	Special Requirements:			Dates Due:		
Notes (Problems, Consultations, Changes, etc.):				Stable Name / Address:		

CLIENT INFORMATION	Name:		
	Address:		
	Phone:		Email:

HORSE INFORMATION	Name:		Breed:
	Gender:		Primary Use:
	Age:		Temperament (1-10):

Veterinarian:	HOOF ANGLES			HOOF LENGTHS		
		Left	Right		Left	Right
Trainer:	Front			Front		
	Back			Back		
Health Concerns:	Supplements:			Shoe Size:		
				Shoe Type:		
				Shoe Pads:		
Therapeutic Treatments:	Special Requirements:			Dates Due:		
Notes (Problems, Consultations, Changes, etc.):				Stable Name / Address:		

CLIENT INFORMATION	Name:	
	Address:	
	Phone:	Email:

HORSE INFORMATION	Name:	Breed:
	Gender:	Primary Use:
	Age:	Temperament (1-10):

Veterinarian:

HOOF ANGLES				HOOF LENGTHS		
	Left	Right			Left	Right
Front				Front		
Back				Back		

Trainer:

Health Concerns:

Supplements:

Shoe Size:	
Shoe Type:	
Shoe Pads:	

Therapeutic Treatments:

Special Requirements:

Dates Due:

Notes (Problems, Consultations, Changes, etc.):

Stable Name / Address:

CLIENT INFORMATION	Name:	
	Address:	
	Phone:	Email:

HORSE INFORMATION	Name:	Breed:
	Gender:	Primary Use:
	Age:	Temperament (1-10):

Veterinarian:

HOOF ANGLES				HOOF LENGTHS		
	Left	Right			Left	Right
Front				Front		
Back				Back		

Trainer:

Health Concerns:

Supplements:

Shoe Size:	
Shoe Type:	
Shoe Pads:	

Therapeutic Treatments:

Special Requirements:

Dates Due:

Notes (Problems, Consultations, Changes, etc.):

Stable Name / Address:

CLIENT INFORMATION	Name:						
	Address:						
	Phone:			Email:			

HORSE INFORMATION	Name:			Breed:			
	Gender:			Primary Use:			
	Age:			Temperament (1-10):			

Veterinarian:	HOOF ANGLES			HOOF LENGTHS		
		Left	Right		Left	Right
Trainer:	Front			Front		
	Back			Back		

Health Concerns:	Supplements:	Shoe Size:
		Shoe Type:
		Shoe Pads:
Therapeutic Treatments:	Special Requirements:	Dates Due:
Notes (Problems, Consultations, Changes, etc.):		Stable Name / Address:

CLIENT INFORMATION	Name:						
	Address:						
	Phone:			Email:			

HORSE INFORMATION	Name:			Breed:			
	Gender:			Primary Use:			
	Age:			Temperament (1-10):			

Veterinarian:	HOOF ANGLES			HOOF LENGTHS		
		Left	Right		Left	Right
Trainer:	Front			Front		
	Back			Back		

Health Concerns:	Supplements:	Shoe Size:
		Shoe Type:
		Shoe Pads:
Therapeutic Treatments:	Special Requirements:	Dates Due:
Notes (Problems, Consultations, Changes, etc.):		Stable Name / Address:

CLIENT INFORMATION	Name:						
	Address:						
	Phone:			Email:			
HORSE INFORMATION	Name:			Breed:			
	Gender:			Primary Use:			
	Age:			Temperament (1-10):			
Veterinarian:	HOOF ANGLES			HOOF LENGTHS			
		Left	Right			Left	Right
Trainer:	Front				Front		
	Back				Back		
Health Concerns:	Supplements:			Shoe Size:			
				Shoe Type:			
				Shoe Pads:			
Therapeutic Treatments:	Special Requirements:			Dates Due:			
Notes (Problems, Consultations, Changes, etc.):				Stable Name / Address:			

CLIENT INFORMATION	Name:						
	Address:						
	Phone:			Email:			
HORSE INFORMATION	Name:			Breed:			
	Gender:			Primary Use:			
	Age:			Temperament (1-10):			
Veterinarian:	HOOF ANGLES			HOOF LENGTHS			
		Left	Right			Left	Right
Trainer:	Front				Front		
	Back				Back		
Health Concerns:	Supplements:			Shoe Size:			
				Shoe Type:			
				Shoe Pads:			
Therapeutic Treatments:	Special Requirements:			Dates Due:			
Notes (Problems, Consultations, Changes, etc.):				Stable Name / Address:			

CLIENT INFORMATION	Name:						
	Address:						
	Phone:				Email:		
HORSE INFORMATION	Name:				Breed:		
	Gender:				Primary Use:		
	Age:				Temperament (1-10):		

Veterinarian:	HOOF ANGLES			HOOF LENGTHS		
		Left	Right		Left	Right
Trainer:	Front			Front		
	Back			Back		
Health Concerns:	Supplements:			Shoe Size:		
				Shoe Type:		
				Shoe Pads:		
Therapeutic Treatments:	Special Requirements:			Dates Due:		
Notes (Problems, Consultations, Changes, etc.):				Stable Name / Address:		

CLIENT INFORMATION	Name:						
	Address:						
	Phone:				Email:		
HORSE INFORMATION	Name:				Breed:		
	Gender:				Primary Use:		
	Age:				Temperament (1-10):		

Veterinarian:	HOOF ANGLES			HOOF LENGTHS		
		Left	Right		Left	Right
Trainer:	Front			Front		
	Back			Back		
Health Concerns:	Supplements:			Shoe Size:		
				Shoe Type:		
				Shoe Pads:		
Therapeutic Treatments:	Special Requirements:			Dates Due:		
Notes (Problems, Consultations, Changes, etc.):				Stable Name / Address:		

CLIENT INFORMATION	Name:						
	Address:						
	Phone:			Email:			
HORSE INFORMATION	Name:			Breed:			
	Gender:			Primary Use:			
	Age:			Temperament (1-10):			

Veterinarian:	HOOF ANGLES			HOOF LENGTHS		
		Left	Right		Left	Right
Trainer:	Front			Front		
	Back			Back		
Health Concerns:	Supplements:			Shoe Size:		
				Shoe Type:		
				Shoe Pads:		
Therapeutic Treatments:	Special Requirements:			Dates Due:		
Notes (Problems, Consultations, Changes, etc.):				Stable Name / Address:		

CLIENT INFORMATION	Name:						
	Address:						
	Phone:			Email:			
HORSE INFORMATION	Name:			Breed:			
	Gender:			Primary Use:			
	Age:			Temperament (1-10):			

Veterinarian:	HOOF ANGLES			HOOF LENGTHS		
		Left	Right		Left	Right
Trainer:	Front			Front		
	Back			Back		
Health Concerns:	Supplements:			Shoe Size:		
				Shoe Type:		
				Shoe Pads:		
Therapeutic Treatments:	Special Requirements:			Dates Due:		
Notes (Problems, Consultations, Changes, etc.):				Stable Name / Address:		

CLIENT INFORMATION	Name:						
	Address:						
	Phone:			Email:			
HORSE INFORMATION	Name:			Breed:			
	Gender:			Primary Use:			
	Age:			Temperament (1-10):			

Veterinarian:	HOOF ANGLES			HOOF LENGTHS		
		Left	Right		Left	Right
Trainer:	Front			Front		
	Back			Back		
Health Concerns:	Supplements:			Shoe Size:		
				Shoe Type:		
				Shoe Pads:		
Therapeutic Treatments:	Special Requirements:			Dates Due:		
Notes (Problems, Consultations, Changes, etc.):				Stable Name / Address:		

CLIENT INFORMATION	Name:						
	Address:						
	Phone:			Email:			
HORSE INFORMATION	Name:			Breed:			
	Gender:			Primary Use:			
	Age:			Temperament (1-10):			

Veterinarian:	HOOF ANGLES			HOOF LENGTHS		
		Left	Right		Left	Right
Trainer:	Front			Front		
	Back			Back		
Health Concerns:	Supplements:			Shoe Size:		
				Shoe Type:		
				Shoe Pads:		
Therapeutic Treatments:	Special Requirements:			Dates Due:		
Notes (Problems, Consultations, Changes, etc.):				Stable Name / Address:		

CLIENT INFORMATION	Name:						
	Address:						
	Phone:			Email:			
HORSE INFORMATION	Name:			Breed:			
	Gender:			Primary Use:			
	Age:			Temperament (1-10):			

Veterinarian:	HOOF ANGLES			HOOF LENGTHS		
		Left	Right		Left	Right
Trainer:	Front			Front		
	Back			Back		
Health Concerns:	Supplements:			Shoe Size:		
				Shoe Type:		
				Shoe Pads:		
Therapeutic Treatments:	Special Requirements:			Dates Due:		
Notes (Problems, Consultations, Changes, etc.):				Stable Name / Address:		

CLIENT INFORMATION	Name:						
	Address:						
	Phone:			Email:			
HORSE INFORMATION	Name:			Breed:			
	Gender:			Primary Use:			
	Age:			Temperament (1-10):			

Veterinarian:	HOOF ANGLES			HOOF LENGTHS		
		Left	Right		Left	Right
Trainer:	Front			Front		
	Back			Back		
Health Concerns:	Supplements:			Shoe Size:		
				Shoe Type:		
				Shoe Pads:		
Therapeutic Treatments:	Special Requirements:			Dates Due:		
Notes (Problems, Consultations, Changes, etc.):				Stable Name / Address:		

CLIENT INFORMATION	Name:					
	Address:					
	Phone:			Email:		
HORSE INFORMATION	Name:			Breed:		
	Gender:			Primary Use:		
	Age:			Temperament (1-10):		

Veterinarian:	HOOF ANGLES			HOOF LENGTHS		
		Left	Right		Left	Right
Trainer:	Front			Front		
	Back			Back		
Health Concerns:	Supplements:			Shoe Size:		
				Shoe Type:		
				Shoe Pads:		
Therapeutic Treatments:	Special Requirements:			Dates Due:		
Notes (Problems, Consultations, Changes, etc.):				Stable Name / Address:		

CLIENT INFORMATION	Name:					
	Address:					
	Phone:			Email:		
HORSE INFORMATION	Name:			Breed:		
	Gender:			Primary Use:		
	Age:			Temperament (1-10):		

Veterinarian:	HOOF ANGLES			HOOF LENGTHS		
		Left	Right		Left	Right
Trainer:	Front			Front		
	Back			Back		
Health Concerns:	Supplements:			Shoe Size:		
				Shoe Type:		
				Shoe Pads:		
Therapeutic Treatments:	Special Requirements:			Dates Due:		
Notes (Problems, Consultations, Changes, etc.):				Stable Name / Address:		

CLIENT INFORMATION	Name:		
	Address:		
	Phone:		Email:

HORSE INFORMATION	Name:		Breed:
	Gender:		Primary Use:
	Age:		Temperament (1-10):

Veterinarian:	HOOF ANGLES			HOOF LENGTHS		
		Left	Right		Left	Right
Trainer:	Front			Front		
	Back			Back		
Health Concerns:	Supplements:			Shoe Size:		
				Shoe Type:		
				Shoe Pads:		
Therapeutic Treatments:	Special Requirements:			Dates Due:		
Notes (Problems, Consultations, Changes, etc.):				Stable Name / Address:		

CLIENT INFORMATION	Name:		
	Address:		
	Phone:		Email:

HORSE INFORMATION	Name:		Breed:
	Gender:		Primary Use:
	Age:		Temperament (1-10):

Veterinarian:	HOOF ANGLES			HOOF LENGTHS		
		Left	Right		Left	Right
Trainer:	Front			Front		
	Back			Back		
Health Concerns:	Supplements:			Shoe Size:		
				Shoe Type:		
				Shoe Pads:		
Therapeutic Treatments:	Special Requirements:			Dates Due:		
Notes (Problems, Consultations, Changes, etc.):				Stable Name / Address:		

CLIENT INFORMATION	Name:		
	Address:		
	Phone:	Email:	

HORSE INFORMATION	Name:	Breed:	
	Gender:	Primary Use:	
	Age:	Temperament (1-10):	

Veterinarian:	HOOF ANGLES			HOOF LENGTHS		
		Left	Right		Left	Right
Trainer:	Front			Front		
	Back			Back		

Health Concerns:	Supplements:	Shoe Size:
		Shoe Type:
		Shoe Pads:
Therapeutic Treatments:	Special Requirements:	Dates Due:

Notes (Problems, Consultations, Changes, etc.):	Stable Name / Address:

CLIENT INFORMATION	Name:		
	Address:		
	Phone:	Email:	

HORSE INFORMATION	Name:	Breed:	
	Gender:	Primary Use:	
	Age:	Temperament (1-10):	

Veterinarian:	HOOF ANGLES			HOOF LENGTHS		
		Left	Right		Left	Right
Trainer:	Front			Front		
	Back			Back		

Health Concerns:	Supplements:	Shoe Size:
		Shoe Type:
		Shoe Pads:
Therapeutic Treatments:	Special Requirements:	Dates Due:

Notes (Problems, Consultations, Changes, etc.):	Stable Name / Address:

CLIENT INFORMATION	Name:		
	Address:		
	Phone:		Email:

HORSE INFORMATION	Name:		Breed:
	Gender:		Primary Use:
	Age:		Temperament (1-10):

Veterinarian:	HOOF ANGLES			HOOF LENGTHS		
		Left	Right		Left	Right
Trainer:	Front			Front		
	Back			Back		

Health Concerns:	Supplements:	Shoe Size:
		Shoe Type:
		Shoe Pads:
Therapeutic Treatments:	Special Requirements:	Dates Due:

| Notes (Problems, Consultations, Changes, etc.): | Stable Name / Address: |

CLIENT INFORMATION	Name:		
	Address:		
	Phone:		Email:

HORSE INFORMATION	Name:		Breed:
	Gender:		Primary Use:
	Age:		Temperament (1-10):

Veterinarian:	HOOF ANGLES			HOOF LENGTHS		
		Left	Right		Left	Right
Trainer:	Front			Front		
	Back			Back		

Health Concerns:	Supplements:	Shoe Size:
		Shoe Type:
		Shoe Pads:
Therapeutic Treatments:	Special Requirements:	Dates Due:

| Notes (Problems, Consultations, Changes, etc.): | Stable Name / Address: |

CLIENT INFORMATION	Name:	
	Address:	
	Phone:	Email:

HORSE INFORMATION	Name:	Breed:
	Gender:	Primary Use:
	Age:	Temperament (1-10):

Veterinarian:	HOOF ANGLES			HOOF LENGTHS		
		Left	Right		Left	Right
Trainer:	Front			Front		
	Back			Back		
Health Concerns:	Supplements:			Shoe Size:		
				Shoe Type:		
				Shoe Pads:		
Therapeutic Treatments:	Special Requirements:			Dates Due:		
Notes (Problems, Consultations, Changes, etc.):				Stable Name / Address:		

CLIENT INFORMATION	Name:	
	Address:	
	Phone:	Email:

HORSE INFORMATION	Name:	Breed:
	Gender:	Primary Use:
	Age:	Temperament (1-10):

Veterinarian:	HOOF ANGLES			HOOF LENGTHS		
		Left	Right		Left	Right
Trainer:	Front			Front		
	Back			Back		
Health Concerns:	Supplements:			Shoe Size:		
				Shoe Type:		
				Shoe Pads:		
Therapeutic Treatments:	Special Requirements:			Dates Due:		
Notes (Problems, Consultations, Changes, etc.):				Stable Name / Address:		

CLIENT INFORMATION	Name:					
	Address:					
	Phone:			Email:		
HORSE INFORMATION	Name:			Breed:		
	Gender:			Primary Use:		
	Age:			Temperament (1-10):		

Veterinarian:	HOOF ANGLES			HOOF LENGTHS		
		Left	Right		Left	Right
Trainer:	Front			Front		
	Back			Back		
Health Concerns:	Supplements:			Shoe Size:		
				Shoe Type:		
				Shoe Pads:		
Therapeutic Treatments:	Special Requirements:			Dates Due:		
Notes (Problems, Consultations, Changes, etc.):				Stable Name / Address:		

CLIENT INFORMATION	Name:					
	Address:					
	Phone:			Email:		
HORSE INFORMATION	Name:			Breed:		
	Gender:			Primary Use:		
	Age:			Temperament (1-10):		

Veterinarian:	HOOF ANGLES			HOOF LENGTHS		
		Left	Right		Left	Right
Trainer:	Front			Front		
	Back			Back		
Health Concerns:	Supplements:			Shoe Size:		
				Shoe Type:		
				Shoe Pads:		
Therapeutic Treatments:	Special Requirements:			Dates Due:		
Notes (Problems, Consultations, Changes, etc.):				Stable Name / Address:		

CLIENT INFORMATION	Name:		
	Address:		
	Phone:	Email:	

HORSE INFORMATION	Name:	Breed:	
	Gender:	Primary Use:	
	Age:	Temperament (1-10):	

Veterinarian:	HOOF ANGLES			HOOF LENGTHS		
		Left	Right		Left	Right
Trainer:	Front			Front		
	Back			Back		

Health Concerns:	Supplements:	Shoe Size:
		Shoe Type:
		Shoe Pads:
Therapeutic Treatments:	Special Requirements:	Dates Due:

Notes (Problems, Consultations, Changes, etc.):	Stable Name / Address:

CLIENT INFORMATION	Name:		
	Address:		
	Phone:	Email:	

HORSE INFORMATION	Name:	Breed:	
	Gender:	Primary Use:	
	Age:	Temperament (1-10):	

Veterinarian:	HOOF ANGLES			HOOF LENGTHS		
		Left	Right		Left	Right
Trainer:	Front			Front		
	Back			Back		

Health Concerns:	Supplements:	Shoe Size:
		Shoe Type:
		Shoe Pads:
Therapeutic Treatments:	Special Requirements:	Dates Due:

Notes (Problems, Consultations, Changes, etc.):	Stable Name / Address:

CLIENT INFORMATION	Name:	
	Address:	
	Phone:	Email:

HORSE INFORMATION	Name:	Breed:
	Gender:	Primary Use:
	Age:	Temperament (1-10):

Veterinarian:

HOOF ANGLES			HOOF LENGTHS		
	Left	Right		Left	Right
Front			Front		
Back			Back		

Trainer:

Health Concerns:	Supplements:	Shoe Size:
		Shoe Type:
		Shoe Pads:
Therapeutic Treatments:	Special Requirements:	Dates Due:

Notes (Problems, Consultations, Changes, etc.):	Stable Name / Address:

CLIENT INFORMATION	Name:	
	Address:	
	Phone:	Email:

HORSE INFORMATION	Name:	Breed:
	Gender:	Primary Use:
	Age:	Temperament (1-10):

Veterinarian:

HOOF ANGLES			HOOF LENGTHS		
	Left	Right		Left	Right
Front			Front		
Back			Back		

Trainer:

Health Concerns:	Supplements:	Shoe Size:
		Shoe Type:
		Shoe Pads:
Therapeutic Treatments:	Special Requirements:	Dates Due:

Notes (Problems, Consultations, Changes, etc.):	Stable Name / Address:

CLIENT INFORMATION	Name:		
	Address:		
	Phone:		Email:

HORSE INFORMATION	Name:		Breed:
	Gender:		Primary Use:
	Age:		Temperament (1-10):

Veterinarian:	HOOF ANGLES			HOOF LENGTHS		
		Left	Right		Left	Right
Trainer:	Front			Front		
	Back			Back		
Health Concerns:	Supplements:			Shoe Size:		
				Shoe Type:		
				Shoe Pads:		
Therapeutic Treatments:	Special Requirements:			Dates Due:		
Notes (Problems, Consultations, Changes, etc.):				Stable Name / Address:		

CLIENT INFORMATION	Name:		
	Address:		
	Phone:		Email:

HORSE INFORMATION	Name:		Breed:
	Gender:		Primary Use:
	Age:		Temperament (1-10):

Veterinarian:	HOOF ANGLES			HOOF LENGTHS		
		Left	Right		Left	Right
Trainer:	Front			Front		
	Back			Back		
Health Concerns:	Supplements:			Shoe Size:		
				Shoe Type:		
				Shoe Pads:		
Therapeutic Treatments:	Special Requirements:			Dates Due:		
Notes (Problems, Consultations, Changes, etc.):				Stable Name / Address:		

CLIENT INFORMATION	Name:		
	Address:		
	Phone:		Email:
HORSE INFORMATION	Name:		Breed:
	Gender:		Primary Use:
	Age:		Temperament (1-10):

Veterinarian:	HOOF ANGLES			HOOF LENGTHS		
		Left	Right		Left	Right
Trainer:	Front			Front		
	Back			Back		
Health Concerns:	Supplements:			Shoe Size:		
				Shoe Type:		
				Shoe Pads:		
Therapeutic Treatments:	Special Requirements:			Dates Due:		
Notes (Problems, Consultations, Changes, etc.):				Stable Name / Address:		

CLIENT INFORMATION	Name:		
	Address:		
	Phone:		Email:
HORSE INFORMATION	Name:		Breed:
	Gender:		Primary Use:
	Age:		Temperament (1-10):

Veterinarian:	HOOF ANGLES			HOOF LENGTHS		
		Left	Right		Left	Right
Trainer:	Front			Front		
	Back			Back		
Health Concerns:	Supplements:			Shoe Size:		
				Shoe Type:		
				Shoe Pads:		
Therapeutic Treatments:	Special Requirements:			Dates Due:		
Notes (Problems, Consultations, Changes, etc.):				Stable Name / Address:		

CLIENT INFORMATION	Name:						
	Address:						
	Phone:				Email:		
HORSE INFORMATION	Name:				Breed:		
	Gender:				Primary Use:		
	Age:				Temperament (1-10):		

Veterinarian:	HOOF ANGLES			HOOF LENGTHS		
		Left	Right		Left	Right
Trainer:	Front			Front		
	Back			Back		
Health Concerns:	Supplements:			Shoe Size:		
				Shoe Type:		
				Shoe Pads:		
Therapeutic Treatments:	Special Requirements:			Dates Due:		
Notes (Problems, Consultations, Changes, etc.):				Stable Name / Address:		

CLIENT INFORMATION	Name:						
	Address:						
	Phone:				Email:		
HORSE INFORMATION	Name:				Breed:		
	Gender:				Primary Use:		
	Age:				Temperament (1-10):		

Veterinarian:	HOOF ANGLES			HOOF LENGTHS		
		Left	Right		Left	Right
Trainer:	Front			Front		
	Back			Back		
Health Concerns:	Supplements:			Shoe Size:		
				Shoe Type:		
				Shoe Pads:		
Therapeutic Treatments:	Special Requirements:			Dates Due:		
Notes (Problems, Consultations, Changes, etc.):				Stable Name / Address:		

CLIENT INFORMATION	Name:				
	Address:				
	Phone:		Email:		

HORSE INFORMATION	Name:			Breed:	
	Gender:			Primary Use:	
	Age:			Temperament (1-10):	

Veterinarian:	HOOF ANGLES			HOOF LENGTHS		
		Left	Right		Left	Right
Trainer:	Front			Front		
	Back			Back		
Health Concerns:	Supplements:			Shoe Size:		
				Shoe Type:		
				Shoe Pads:		
Therapeutic Treatments:	Special Requirements:			Dates Due:		
Notes (Problems, Consultations, Changes, etc.):				Stable Name / Address:		

CLIENT INFORMATION	Name:				
	Address:				
	Phone:		Email:		

HORSE INFORMATION	Name:			Breed:	
	Gender:			Primary Use:	
	Age:			Temperament (1-10):	

Veterinarian:	HOOF ANGLES			HOOF LENGTHS		
		Left	Right		Left	Right
Trainer:	Front			Front		
	Back			Back		
Health Concerns:	Supplements:			Shoe Size:		
				Shoe Type:		
				Shoe Pads:		
Therapeutic Treatments:	Special Requirements:			Dates Due:		
Notes (Problems, Consultations, Changes, etc.):				Stable Name / Address:		

CLIENT INFORMATION	Name:						
	Address:						
	Phone:				Email:		
HORSE INFORMATION	Name:				Breed:		
	Gender:				Primary Use:		
	Age:				Temperament (1-10):		

Veterinarian:	HOOF ANGLES			HOOF LENGTHS		
		Left	Right		Left	Right
Trainer:	Front			Front		
	Back			Back		
Health Concerns:	Supplements:			Shoe Size:		
				Shoe Type:		
				Shoe Pads:		
Therapeutic Treatments:	Special Requirements:			Dates Due:		
Notes (Problems, Consultations, Changes, etc.):				Stable Name / Address:		

CLIENT INFORMATION	Name:						
	Address:						
	Phone:				Email:		
HORSE INFORMATION	Name:				Breed:		
	Gender:				Primary Use:		
	Age:				Temperament (1-10):		

Veterinarian:	HOOF ANGLES			HOOF LENGTHS		
		Left	Right		Left	Right
Trainer:	Front			Front		
	Back			Back		
Health Concerns:	Supplements:			Shoe Size:		
				Shoe Type:		
				Shoe Pads:		
Therapeutic Treatments:	Special Requirements:			Dates Due:		
Notes (Problems, Consultations, Changes, etc.):				Stable Name / Address:		

CLIENT INFORMATION	Name:						
	Address:						
	Phone:				Email:		
HORSE INFORMATION	Name:				Breed:		
	Gender:				Primary Use:		
	Age:				Temperament (1-10):		

Veterinarian:	HOOF ANGLES			HOOF LENGTHS		
		Left	Right		Left	Right
Trainer:	Front			Front		
	Back			Back		
Health Concerns:	Supplements:			Shoe Size:		
				Shoe Type:		
				Shoe Pads:		
Therapeutic Treatments:	Special Requirements:			Dates Due:		
Notes (Problems, Consultations, Changes, etc.):				Stable Name / Address:		

CLIENT INFORMATION	Name:						
	Address:						
	Phone:				Email:		
HORSE INFORMATION	Name:				Breed:		
	Gender:				Primary Use:		
	Age:				Temperament (1-10):		

Veterinarian:	HOOF ANGLES			HOOF LENGTHS		
		Left	Right		Left	Right
Trainer:	Front			Front		
	Back			Back		
Health Concerns:	Supplements:			Shoe Size:		
				Shoe Type:		
				Shoe Pads:		
Therapeutic Treatments:	Special Requirements:			Dates Due:		
Notes (Problems, Consultations, Changes, etc.):				Stable Name / Address:		

CLIENT INFORMATION	Name:	
	Address:	
	Phone:	Email:
HORSE INFORMATION	Name:	Breed:
	Gender:	Primary Use:
	Age:	Temperament (1-10):

Veterinarian:	HOOF ANGLES			HOOF LENGTHS		
		Left	Right		Left	Right
Trainer:	Front			Front		
	Back			Back		
Health Concerns:	Supplements:			Shoe Size:		
				Shoe Type:		
				Shoe Pads:		
Therapeutic Treatments:	Special Requirements:			Dates Due:		
Notes (Problems, Consultations, Changes, etc.):				Stable Name / Address:		

CLIENT INFORMATION	Name:	
	Address:	
	Phone:	Email:
HORSE INFORMATION	Name:	Breed:
	Gender:	Primary Use:
	Age:	Temperament (1-10):

Veterinarian:	HOOF ANGLES			HOOF LENGTHS		
		Left	Right		Left	Right
Trainer:	Front			Front		
	Back			Back		
Health Concerns:	Supplements:			Shoe Size:		
				Shoe Type:		
				Shoe Pads:		
Therapeutic Treatments:	Special Requirements:			Dates Due:		
Notes (Problems, Consultations, Changes, etc.):				Stable Name / Address:		

CLIENT INFORMATION	Name:						
	Address:						
	Phone:			Email:			
HORSE INFORMATION	Name:			Breed:			
	Gender:			Primary Use:			
	Age:			Temperament (1-10):			
Veterinarian:	HOOF ANGLES			HOOF LENGTHS			
		Left	Right			Left	Right
Trainer:	Front				Front		
	Back				Back		
Health Concerns:	Supplements:			Shoe Size:			
				Shoe Type:			
				Shoe Pads:			
Therapeutic Treatments:	Special Requirements:			Dates Due:			
Notes (Problems, Consultations, Changes, etc.):				Stable Name / Address:			

CLIENT INFORMATION	Name:						
	Address:						
	Phone:			Email:			
HORSE INFORMATION	Name:			Breed:			
	Gender:			Primary Use:			
	Age:			Temperament (1-10):			
Veterinarian:	HOOF ANGLES			HOOF LENGTHS			
		Left	Right			Left	Right
Trainer:	Front				Front		
	Back				Back		
Health Concerns:	Supplements:			Shoe Size:			
				Shoe Type:			
				Shoe Pads:			
Therapeutic Treatments:	Special Requirements:			Dates Due:			
Notes (Problems, Consultations, Changes, etc.):				Stable Name / Address:			

CLIENT INFORMATION	Name:	
	Address:	
	Phone:	Email:
HORSE INFORMATION	Name:	Breed:
	Gender:	Primary Use:
	Age:	Temperament (1-10):

Veterinarian:	HOOF ANGLES			HOOF LENGTHS		
		Left	Right		Left	Right
Trainer:	Front			Front		
	Back			Back		
Health Concerns:	Supplements:			Shoe Size:		
				Shoe Type:		
				Shoe Pads:		
Therapeutic Treatments:	Special Requirements:			Dates Due:		
Notes (Problems, Consultations, Changes, etc.):				Stable Name / Address:		

CLIENT INFORMATION	Name:	
	Address:	
	Phone:	Email:
HORSE INFORMATION	Name:	Breed:
	Gender:	Primary Use:
	Age:	Temperament (1-10):

Veterinarian:	HOOF ANGLES			HOOF LENGTHS		
		Left	Right		Left	Right
Trainer:	Front			Front		
	Back			Back		
Health Concerns:	Supplements:			Shoe Size:		
				Shoe Type:		
				Shoe Pads:		
Therapeutic Treatments:	Special Requirements:			Dates Due:		
Notes (Problems, Consultations, Changes, etc.):				Stable Name / Address:		

CLIENT INFORMATION	Name:						
	Address:						
	Phone:			Email:			
HORSE INFORMATION	Name:			Breed:			
	Gender:			Primary Use:			
	Age:			Temperament (1-10):			

Veterinarian:	HOOF ANGLES			HOOF LENGTHS		
		Left	Right		Left	Right
Trainer:	Front			Front		
	Back			Back		
Health Concerns:	Supplements:			Shoe Size:		
				Shoe Type:		
				Shoe Pads:		
Therapeutic Treatments:	Special Requirements:			Dates Due:		
Notes (Problems, Consultations, Changes, etc.):				Stable Name / Address:		

CLIENT INFORMATION	Name:						
	Address:						
	Phone:			Email:			
HORSE INFORMATION	Name:			Breed:			
	Gender:			Primary Use:			
	Age:			Temperament (1-10):			

Veterinarian:	HOOF ANGLES			HOOF LENGTHS		
		Left	Right		Left	Right
Trainer:	Front			Front		
	Back			Back		
Health Concerns:	Supplements:			Shoe Size:		
				Shoe Type:		
				Shoe Pads:		
Therapeutic Treatments:	Special Requirements:			Dates Due:		
Notes (Problems, Consultations, Changes, etc.):				Stable Name / Address:		

CLIENT INFORMATION	Name:						
	Address:						
	Phone:				Email:		
HORSE INFORMATION	Name:				Breed:		
	Gender:				Primary Use:		
	Age:				Temperament (1-10):		

Veterinarian:	HOOF ANGLES			HOOF LENGTHS		
		Left	Right		Left	Right
Trainer:	Front			Front		
	Back			Back		
Health Concerns:	Supplements:			Shoe Size:		
				Shoe Type:		
				Shoe Pads:		
Therapeutic Treatments:	Special Requirements:			Dates Due:		
Notes (Problems, Consultations, Changes, etc.):				Stable Name / Address:		

CLIENT INFORMATION	Name:						
	Address:						
	Phone:				Email:		
HORSE INFORMATION	Name:				Breed:		
	Gender:				Primary Use:		
	Age:				Temperament (1-10):		

Veterinarian:	HOOF ANGLES			HOOF LENGTHS		
		Left	Right		Left	Right
Trainer:	Front			Front		
	Back			Back		
Health Concerns:	Supplements:			Shoe Size:		
				Shoe Type:		
				Shoe Pads:		
Therapeutic Treatments:	Special Requirements:			Dates Due:		
Notes (Problems, Consultations, Changes, etc.):				Stable Name / Address:		

CLIENT INFORMATION	Name:						
	Address:						
	Phone:			Email:			
HORSE INFORMATION	Name:			Breed:			
	Gender:			Primary Use:			
	Age:			Temperament (1-10):			

Veterinarian:	HOOF ANGLES			HOOF LENGTHS		
		Left	Right		Left	Right
Trainer:	Front			Front		
	Back			Back		

Health Concerns:	Supplements:	Shoe Size:
		Shoe Type:
		Shoe Pads:
Therapeutic Treatments:	Special Requirements:	Dates Due:

Notes (Problems, Consultations, Changes, etc.):	Stable Name / Address:

CLIENT INFORMATION	Name:						
	Address:						
	Phone:			Email:			
HORSE INFORMATION	Name:			Breed:			
	Gender:			Primary Use:			
	Age:			Temperament (1-10):			

Veterinarian:	HOOF ANGLES			HOOF LENGTHS		
		Left	Right		Left	Right
Trainer:	Front			Front		
	Back			Back		

Health Concerns:	Supplements:	Shoe Size:
		Shoe Type:
		Shoe Pads:
Therapeutic Treatments:	Special Requirements:	Dates Due:

Notes (Problems, Consultations, Changes, etc.):	Stable Name / Address:

CLIENT INFORMATION	Name:		
	Address:		
	Phone:		Email:

HORSE INFORMATION	Name:		Breed:
	Gender:		Primary Use:
	Age:		Temperament (1-10):

Veterinarian:	HOOF ANGLES			HOOF LENGTHS		
		Left	Right		Left	Right
Trainer:	Front			Front		
	Back			Back		
Health Concerns:	Supplements:			Shoe Size:		
				Shoe Type:		
				Shoe Pads:		
Therapeutic Treatments:	Special Requirements:			Dates Due:		
Notes (Problems, Consultations, Changes, etc.):				Stable Name / Address:		

CLIENT INFORMATION	Name:		
	Address:		
	Phone:		Email:

HORSE INFORMATION	Name:		Breed:
	Gender:		Primary Use:
	Age:		Temperament (1-10):

Veterinarian:	HOOF ANGLES			HOOF LENGTHS		
		Left	Right		Left	Right
Trainer:	Front			Front		
	Back			Back		
Health Concerns:	Supplements:			Shoe Size:		
				Shoe Type:		
				Shoe Pads:		
Therapeutic Treatments:	Special Requirements:			Dates Due:		
Notes (Problems, Consultations, Changes, etc.):				Stable Name / Address:		

CLIENT INFORMATION	Name:		
	Address:		
	Phone:		Email:
HORSE INFORMATION	Name:		Breed:
	Gender:		Primary Use:
	Age:		Temperament (1-10):

Veterinarian:	HOOF ANGLES			HOOF LENGTHS		
		Left	Right		Left	Right
Trainer:	Front			Front		
	Back			Back		
Health Concerns:	Supplements:			Shoe Size:		
				Shoe Type:		
				Shoe Pads:		
Therapeutic Treatments:	Special Requirements:			Dates Due:		
Notes (Problems, Consultations, Changes, etc.):				Stable Name / Address:		

CLIENT INFORMATION	Name:		
	Address:		
	Phone:		Email:
HORSE INFORMATION	Name:		Breed:
	Gender:		Primary Use:
	Age:		Temperament (1-10):

Veterinarian:	HOOF ANGLES			HOOF LENGTHS		
		Left	Right		Left	Right
Trainer:	Front			Front		
	Back			Back		
Health Concerns:	Supplements:			Shoe Size:		
				Shoe Type:		
				Shoe Pads:		
Therapeutic Treatments:	Special Requirements:			Dates Due:		
Notes (Problems, Consultations, Changes, etc.):				Stable Name / Address:		

CLIENT INFORMATION	Name:		
	Address:		
	Phone:		Email:

HORSE INFORMATION	Name:		Breed:
	Gender:		Primary Use:
	Age:		Temperament (1-10):

Veterinarian:	HOOF ANGLES			HOOF LENGTHS		
		Left	Right		Left	Right
Trainer:	Front			Front		
	Back			Back		
Health Concerns:	Supplements:			Shoe Size:		
				Shoe Type:		
				Shoe Pads:		
Therapeutic Treatments:	Special Requirements:			Dates Due:		
Notes (Problems, Consultations, Changes, etc.):				Stable Name / Address:		

CLIENT INFORMATION	Name:		
	Address:		
	Phone:		Email:

HORSE INFORMATION	Name:		Breed:
	Gender:		Primary Use:
	Age:		Temperament (1-10):

Veterinarian:	HOOF ANGLES			HOOF LENGTHS		
		Left	Right		Left	Right
Trainer:	Front			Front		
	Back			Back		
Health Concerns:	Supplements:			Shoe Size:		
				Shoe Type:		
				Shoe Pads:		
Therapeutic Treatments:	Special Requirements:			Dates Due:		
Notes (Problems, Consultations, Changes, etc.):				Stable Name / Address:		

CLIENT INFORMATION	Name:	
	Address:	
	Phone:	Email:

HORSE INFORMATION	Name:	Breed:
	Gender:	Primary Use:
	Age:	Temperament (1-10):

Veterinarian:	HOOF ANGLES			HOOF LENGTHS		
		Left	Right		Left	Right
Trainer:	Front			Front		
	Back			Back		
Health Concerns:	Supplements:			Shoe Size:		
				Shoe Type:		
				Shoe Pads:		
Therapeutic Treatments:	Special Requirements:			Dates Due:		
Notes (Problems, Consultations, Changes, etc.):				Stable Name / Address:		

CLIENT INFORMATION	Name:	
	Address:	
	Phone:	Email:

HORSE INFORMATION	Name:	Breed:
	Gender:	Primary Use:
	Age:	Temperament (1-10):

Veterinarian:	HOOF ANGLES			HOOF LENGTHS		
		Left	Right		Left	Right
Trainer:	Front			Front		
	Back			Back		
Health Concerns:	Supplements:			Shoe Size:		
				Shoe Type:		
				Shoe Pads:		
Therapeutic Treatments:	Special Requirements:			Dates Due:		
Notes (Problems, Consultations, Changes, etc.):				Stable Name / Address:		

CLIENT INFORMATION	Name:						
	Address:						
	Phone:			Email:			
HORSE INFORMATION	Name:			Breed:			
	Gender:			Primary Use:			
	Age:			Temperament (1-10):			

Veterinarian:	HOOF ANGLES			HOOF LENGTHS		
		Left	Right		Left	Right
Trainer:	Front			Front		
	Back			Back		
Health Concerns:	Supplements:			Shoe Size:		
				Shoe Type:		
				Shoe Pads:		
Therapeutic Treatments:	Special Requirements:			Dates Due:		
Notes (Problems, Consultations, Changes, etc.):				Stable Name / Address:		

CLIENT INFORMATION	Name:						
	Address:						
	Phone:			Email:			
HORSE INFORMATION	Name:			Breed:			
	Gender:			Primary Use:			
	Age:			Temperament (1-10):			

Veterinarian:	HOOF ANGLES			HOOF LENGTHS		
		Left	Right		Left	Right
Trainer:	Front			Front		
	Back			Back		
Health Concerns:	Supplements:			Shoe Size:		
				Shoe Type:		
				Shoe Pads:		
Therapeutic Treatments:	Special Requirements:			Dates Due:		
Notes (Problems, Consultations, Changes, etc.):				Stable Name / Address:		

CLIENT INFORMATION	Name:	
	Address:	
	Phone:	Email:

HORSE INFORMATION	Name:	Breed:
	Gender:	Primary Use:
	Age:	Temperament (1-10):

Veterinarian:	HOOF ANGLES			HOOF LENGTHS		
		Left	Right		Left	Right
Trainer:	Front			Front		
	Back			Back		
Health Concerns:	Supplements:			Shoe Size:		
				Shoe Type:		
				Shoe Pads:		
Therapeutic Treatments:	Special Requirements:			Dates Due:		
Notes (Problems, Consultations, Changes, etc.):				Stable Name / Address:		

CLIENT INFORMATION	Name:	
	Address:	
	Phone:	Email:

HORSE INFORMATION	Name:	Breed:
	Gender:	Primary Use:
	Age:	Temperament (1-10):

Veterinarian:	HOOF ANGLES			HOOF LENGTHS		
		Left	Right		Left	Right
Trainer:	Front			Front		
	Back			Back		
Health Concerns:	Supplements:			Shoe Size:		
				Shoe Type:		
				Shoe Pads:		
Therapeutic Treatments:	Special Requirements:			Dates Due:		
Notes (Problems, Consultations, Changes, etc.):				Stable Name / Address:		

CLIENT INFORMATION	Name:	
	Address:	
	Phone:	Email:

HORSE INFORMATION	Name:	Breed:
	Gender:	Primary Use:
	Age:	Temperament (1-10):

Veterinarian:	HOOF ANGLES			HOOF LENGTHS		
		Left	Right		Left	Right
Trainer:	Front			Front		
	Back			Back		
Health Concerns:	Supplements:			Shoe Size:		
				Shoe Type:		
				Shoe Pads:		
Therapeutic Treatments:	Special Requirements:			Dates Due:		
Notes (Problems, Consultations, Changes, etc.):				Stable Name / Address:		

CLIENT INFORMATION	Name:	
	Address:	
	Phone:	Email:

HORSE INFORMATION	Name:	Breed:
	Gender:	Primary Use:
	Age:	Temperament (1-10):

Veterinarian:	HOOF ANGLES			HOOF LENGTHS		
		Left	Right		Left	Right
Trainer:	Front			Front		
	Back			Back		
Health Concerns:	Supplements:			Shoe Size:		
				Shoe Type:		
				Shoe Pads:		
Therapeutic Treatments:	Special Requirements:			Dates Due:		
Notes (Problems, Consultations, Changes, etc.):				Stable Name / Address:		

CLIENT INFORMATION	Name:		
	Address:		
	Phone:	Email:	

HORSE INFORMATION	Name:	Breed:	
	Gender:	Primary Use:	
	Age:	Temperament (1-10):	

Veterinarian:	HOOF ANGLES			HOOF LENGTHS		
		Left	Right		Left	Right
Trainer:	Front			Front		
	Back			Back		

Health Concerns:	Supplements:	Shoe Size:
		Shoe Type:
		Shoe Pads:
Therapeutic Treatments:	Special Requirements:	Dates Due:
Notes (Problems, Consultations, Changes, etc.):		Stable Name / Address:

CLIENT INFORMATION	Name:		
	Address:		
	Phone:	Email:	

HORSE INFORMATION	Name:	Breed:	
	Gender:	Primary Use:	
	Age:	Temperament (1-10):	

Veterinarian:	HOOF ANGLES			HOOF LENGTHS		
		Left	Right		Left	Right
Trainer:	Front			Front		
	Back			Back		

Health Concerns:	Supplements:	Shoe Size:
		Shoe Type:
		Shoe Pads:
Therapeutic Treatments:	Special Requirements:	Dates Due:
Notes (Problems, Consultations, Changes, etc.):		Stable Name / Address:

CLIENT INFORMATION	Name:		
	Address:		
	Phone:		Email:

HORSE INFORMATION	Name:		Breed:
	Gender:		Primary Use:
	Age:		Temperament (1-10):

Veterinarian:	HOOF ANGLES			HOOF LENGTHS		
		Left	Right		Left	Right
Trainer:	Front			Front		
	Back			Back		
Health Concerns:	Supplements:			Shoe Size:		
				Shoe Type:		
				Shoe Pads:		
Therapeutic Treatments:	Special Requirements:			Dates Due:		
Notes (Problems, Consultations, Changes, etc.):				Stable Name / Address:		

CLIENT INFORMATION	Name:		
	Address:		
	Phone:		Email:

HORSE INFORMATION	Name:		Breed:
	Gender:		Primary Use:
	Age:		Temperament (1-10):

Veterinarian:	HOOF ANGLES			HOOF LENGTHS		
		Left	Right		Left	Right
Trainer:	Front			Front		
	Back			Back		
Health Concerns:	Supplements:			Shoe Size:		
				Shoe Type:		
				Shoe Pads:		
Therapeutic Treatments:	Special Requirements:			Dates Due:		
Notes (Problems, Consultations, Changes, etc.):				Stable Name / Address:		

CLIENT INFORMATION	Name:		
	Address:		
	Phone:	Email:	

HORSE INFORMATION	Name:	Breed:	
	Gender:	Primary Use:	
	Age:	Temperament (1-10):	

Veterinarian:	HOOF ANGLES			HOOF LENGTHS		
		Left	Right		Left	Right
Trainer:	Front			Front		
	Back			Back		

Health Concerns:	Supplements:	Shoe Size:
		Shoe Type:
		Shoe Pads:
Therapeutic Treatments:	Special Requirements:	Dates Due:
Notes (Problems, Consultations, Changes, etc.):		Stable Name / Address:

CLIENT INFORMATION	Name:		
	Address:		
	Phone:	Email:	

HORSE INFORMATION	Name:	Breed:	
	Gender:	Primary Use:	
	Age:	Temperament (1-10):	

Veterinarian:	HOOF ANGLES			HOOF LENGTHS		
		Left	Right		Left	Right
Trainer:	Front			Front		
	Back			Back		

Health Concerns:	Supplements:	Shoe Size:
		Shoe Type:
		Shoe Pads:
Therapeutic Treatments:	Special Requirements:	Dates Due:
Notes (Problems, Consultations, Changes, etc.):		Stable Name / Address:

CLIENT INFORMATION	Name:						
	Address:						
	Phone:			Email:			
HORSE INFORMATION	Name:			Breed:			
	Gender:			Primary Use:			
	Age:			Temperament (1-10):			

Veterinarian:	HOOF ANGLES			HOOF LENGTHS		
		Left	Right		Left	Right
Trainer:	Front			Front		
	Back			Back		

Health Concerns:	Supplements:	Shoe Size:
		Shoe Type:
		Shoe Pads:
Therapeutic Treatments:	Special Requirements:	Dates Due:
Notes (Problems, Consultations, Changes, etc.):		Stable Name / Address:

CLIENT INFORMATION	Name:						
	Address:						
	Phone:			Email:			
HORSE INFORMATION	Name:			Breed:			
	Gender:			Primary Use:			
	Age:			Temperament (1-10):			

Veterinarian:	HOOF ANGLES			HOOF LENGTHS		
		Left	Right		Left	Right
Trainer:	Front			Front		
	Back			Back		

Health Concerns:	Supplements:	Shoe Size:
		Shoe Type:
		Shoe Pads:
Therapeutic Treatments:	Special Requirements:	Dates Due:
Notes (Problems, Consultations, Changes, etc.):		Stable Name / Address:

CLIENT INFORMATION	Name:			
	Address:			
	Phone:		Email:	

HORSE INFORMATION	Name:		Breed:	
	Gender:		Primary Use:	
	Age:		Temperament (1-10):	

Veterinarian:	HOOF ANGLES			HOOF LENGTHS		
		Left	Right		Left	Right
Trainer:	Front			Front		
	Back			Back		
Health Concerns:	Supplements:			Shoe Size:		
				Shoe Type:		
				Shoe Pads:		
Therapeutic Treatments:	Special Requirements:			Dates Due:		
Notes (Problems, Consultations, Changes, etc.):				Stable Name / Address:		

CLIENT INFORMATION	Name:			
	Address:			
	Phone:		Email:	

HORSE INFORMATION	Name:		Breed:	
	Gender:		Primary Use:	
	Age:		Temperament (1-10):	

Veterinarian:	HOOF ANGLES			HOOF LENGTHS		
		Left	Right		Left	Right
Trainer:	Front			Front		
	Back			Back		
Health Concerns:	Supplements:			Shoe Size:		
				Shoe Type:		
				Shoe Pads:		
Therapeutic Treatments:	Special Requirements:			Dates Due:		
Notes (Problems, Consultations, Changes, etc.):				Stable Name / Address:		

CLIENT INFORMATION	Name:	
	Address:	
	Phone:	Email:

HORSE INFORMATION	Name:	Breed:
	Gender:	Primary Use:
	Age:	Temperament (1-10):

Veterinarian:	HOOF ANGLES			HOOF LENGTHS		
		Left	Right		Left	Right
Trainer:	Front			Front		
	Back			Back		
Health Concerns:	Supplements:			Shoe Size:		
				Shoe Type:		
				Shoe Pads:		
Therapeutic Treatments:	Special Requirements:			Dates Due:		
Notes (Problems, Consultations, Changes, etc.):				Stable Name / Address:		

CLIENT INFORMATION	Name:	
	Address:	
	Phone:	Email:

HORSE INFORMATION	Name:	Breed:
	Gender:	Primary Use:
	Age:	Temperament (1-10):

Veterinarian:	HOOF ANGLES			HOOF LENGTHS		
		Left	Right		Left	Right
Trainer:	Front			Front		
	Back			Back		
Health Concerns:	Supplements:			Shoe Size:		
				Shoe Type:		
				Shoe Pads:		
Therapeutic Treatments:	Special Requirements:			Dates Due:		
Notes (Problems, Consultations, Changes, etc.):				Stable Name / Address:		

CLIENT INFORMATION	Name:						
	Address:						
	Phone:			Email:			
HORSE INFORMATION	Name:			Breed:			
	Gender:			Primary Use:			
	Age:			Temperament (1-10):			

Veterinarian:	HOOF ANGLES			HOOF LENGTHS		
		Left	Right		Left	Right
Trainer:	Front			Front		
	Back			Back		

Health Concerns:	Supplements:	Shoe Size:
		Shoe Type:
		Shoe Pads:
Therapeutic Treatments:	Special Requirements:	Dates Due:
Notes (Problems, Consultations, Changes, etc.):		Stable Name / Address:

CLIENT INFORMATION	Name:						
	Address:						
	Phone:			Email:			
HORSE INFORMATION	Name:			Breed:			
	Gender:			Primary Use:			
	Age:			Temperament (1-10):			

Veterinarian:	HOOF ANGLES			HOOF LENGTHS		
		Left	Right		Left	Right
Trainer:	Front			Front		
	Back			Back		

Health Concerns:	Supplements:	Shoe Size:
		Shoe Type:
		Shoe Pads:
Therapeutic Treatments:	Special Requirements:	Dates Due:
Notes (Problems, Consultations, Changes, etc.):		Stable Name / Address:

CLIENT INFORMATION	Name:						
	Address:						
	Phone:			Email:			
HORSE INFORMATION	Name:			Breed:			
	Gender:			Primary Use:			
	Age:			Temperament (1-10):			

Veterinarian:	HOOF ANGLES			HOOF LENGTHS		
		Left	Right		Left	Right
Trainer:	Front			Front		
	Back			Back		

Health Concerns:	Supplements:	Shoe Size:
		Shoe Type:
		Shoe Pads:
Therapeutic Treatments:	Special Requirements:	Dates Due:
Notes (Problems, Consultations, Changes, etc.):		Stable Name / Address:

CLIENT INFORMATION	Name:						
	Address:						
	Phone:			Email:			
HORSE INFORMATION	Name:			Breed:			
	Gender:			Primary Use:			
	Age:			Temperament (1-10):			

Veterinarian:	HOOF ANGLES			HOOF LENGTHS		
		Left	Right		Left	Right
Trainer:	Front			Front		
	Back			Back		

Health Concerns:	Supplements:	Shoe Size:
		Shoe Type:
		Shoe Pads:
Therapeutic Treatments:	Special Requirements:	Dates Due:
Notes (Problems, Consultations, Changes, etc.):		Stable Name / Address:

CLIENT INFORMATION	Name:		
	Address:		
	Phone:		Email:

HORSE INFORMATION	Name:		Breed:
	Gender:		Primary Use:
	Age:		Temperament (1-10):

Veterinarian:	HOOF ANGLES			HOOF LENGTHS		
		Left	Right		Left	Right
Trainer:	Front			Front		
	Back			Back		
Health Concerns:	Supplements:			Shoe Size:		
				Shoe Type:		
				Shoe Pads:		
Therapeutic Treatments:	Special Requirements:			Dates Due:		
Notes (Problems, Consultations, Changes, etc.):				Stable Name / Address:		

CLIENT INFORMATION	Name:		
	Address:		
	Phone:		Email:

HORSE INFORMATION	Name:		Breed:
	Gender:		Primary Use:
	Age:		Temperament (1-10):

Veterinarian:	HOOF ANGLES			HOOF LENGTHS		
		Left	Right		Left	Right
Trainer:	Front			Front		
	Back			Back		
Health Concerns:	Supplements:			Shoe Size:		
				Shoe Type:		
				Shoe Pads:		
Therapeutic Treatments:	Special Requirements:			Dates Due:		
Notes (Problems, Consultations, Changes, etc.):				Stable Name / Address:		

CLIENT INFORMATION	Name:	
	Address:	
	Phone:	Email:

HORSE INFORMATION	Name:	Breed:
	Gender:	Primary Use:
	Age:	Temperament (1-10):

Veterinarian:	HOOF ANGLES			HOOF LENGTHS		
		Left	Right		Left	Right
Trainer:	Front			Front		
	Back			Back		
Health Concerns:	Supplements:			Shoe Size:		
				Shoe Type:		
				Shoe Pads:		
Therapeutic Treatments:	Special Requirements:			Dates Due:		
Notes (Problems, Consultations, Changes, etc.):				Stable Name / Address:		

CLIENT INFORMATION	Name:	
	Address:	
	Phone:	Email:

HORSE INFORMATION	Name:	Breed:
	Gender:	Primary Use:
	Age:	Temperament (1-10):

Veterinarian:	HOOF ANGLES			HOOF LENGTHS		
		Left	Right		Left	Right
Trainer:	Front			Front		
	Back			Back		
Health Concerns:	Supplements:			Shoe Size:		
				Shoe Type:		
				Shoe Pads:		
Therapeutic Treatments:	Special Requirements:			Dates Due:		
Notes (Problems, Consultations, Changes, etc.):				Stable Name / Address:		

CLIENT INFORMATION	Name:						
	Address:						
	Phone:				Email:		

HORSE INFORMATION	Name:				Breed:		
	Gender:				Primary Use:		
	Age:				Temperament (1-10):		

Veterinarian:	HOOF ANGLES			HOOF LENGTHS		
		Left	Right		Left	Right
Trainer:	Front			Front		
	Back			Back		

Health Concerns:	Supplements:	Shoe Size:
		Shoe Type:
		Shoe Pads:
Therapeutic Treatments:	Special Requirements:	Dates Due:

Notes (Problems, Consultations, Changes, etc.):	Stable Name / Address:

CLIENT INFORMATION	Name:						
	Address:						
	Phone:				Email:		

HORSE INFORMATION	Name:				Breed:		
	Gender:				Primary Use:		
	Age:				Temperament (1-10):		

Veterinarian:	HOOF ANGLES			HOOF LENGTHS		
		Left	Right		Left	Right
Trainer:	Front			Front		
	Back			Back		

Health Concerns:	Supplements:	Shoe Size:
		Shoe Type:
		Shoe Pads:
Therapeutic Treatments:	Special Requirements:	Dates Due:

Notes (Problems, Consultations, Changes, etc.):	Stable Name / Address:

CLIENT INFORMATION	Name:	
	Address:	
	Phone:	Email:

HORSE INFORMATION	Name:	Breed:
	Gender:	Primary Use:
	Age:	Temperament (1-10):

Veterinarian:	HOOF ANGLES			HOOF LENGTHS		
		Left	Right		Left	Right
Trainer:	Front			Front		
	Back			Back		

Health Concerns:	Supplements:	Shoe Size:
		Shoe Type:
		Shoe Pads:
Therapeutic Treatments:	Special Requirements:	Dates Due:

| Notes (Problems, Consultations, Changes, etc.): | Stable Name / Address: |

CLIENT INFORMATION	Name:	
	Address:	
	Phone:	Email:

HORSE INFORMATION	Name:	Breed:
	Gender:	Primary Use:
	Age:	Temperament (1-10):

Veterinarian:	HOOF ANGLES			HOOF LENGTHS		
		Left	Right		Left	Right
Trainer:	Front			Front		
	Back			Back		

Health Concerns:	Supplements:	Shoe Size:
		Shoe Type:
		Shoe Pads:
Therapeutic Treatments:	Special Requirements:	Dates Due:

| Notes (Problems, Consultations, Changes, etc.): | Stable Name / Address: |

CLIENT INFORMATION	Name:						
	Address:						
	Phone:			Email:			
HORSE INFORMATION	Name:			Breed:			
	Gender:			Primary Use:			
	Age:			Temperament (1-10):			
Veterinarian:	HOOF ANGLES			HOOF LENGTHS			
		Left	Right			Left	Right
Trainer:	Front				Front		
	Back				Back		
Health Concerns:	Supplements:			Shoe Size:			
				Shoe Type:			
				Shoe Pads:			
Therapeutic Treatments:	Special Requirements:			Dates Due:			
Notes (Problems, Consultations, Changes, etc.):				Stable Name / Address:			

CLIENT INFORMATION	Name:						
	Address:						
	Phone:			Email:			
HORSE INFORMATION	Name:			Breed:			
	Gender:			Primary Use:			
	Age:			Temperament (1-10):			
Veterinarian:	HOOF ANGLES			HOOF LENGTHS			
		Left	Right			Left	Right
Trainer:	Front				Front		
	Back				Back		
Health Concerns:	Supplements:			Shoe Size:			
				Shoe Type:			
				Shoe Pads:			
Therapeutic Treatments:	Special Requirements:			Dates Due:			
Notes (Problems, Consultations, Changes, etc.):				Stable Name / Address:			

CLIENT INFORMATION	Name:						
	Address:						
	Phone:				Email:		

HORSE INFORMATION	Name:				Breed:		
	Gender:				Primary Use:		
	Age:				Temperament (1-10):		

Veterinarian:	HOOF ANGLES			HOOF LENGTHS		
		Left	Right		Left	Right
Trainer:	Front			Front		
	Back			Back		
Health Concerns:	Supplements:			Shoe Size:		
				Shoe Type:		
				Shoe Pads:		
Therapeutic Treatments:	Special Requirements:			Dates Due:		
Notes (Problems, Consultations, Changes, etc.):				Stable Name / Address:		

CLIENT INFORMATION	Name:						
	Address:						
	Phone:				Email:		

HORSE INFORMATION	Name:				Breed:		
	Gender:				Primary Use:		
	Age:				Temperament (1-10):		

Veterinarian:	HOOF ANGLES			HOOF LENGTHS		
		Left	Right		Left	Right
Trainer:	Front			Front		
	Back			Back		
Health Concerns:	Supplements:			Shoe Size:		
				Shoe Type:		
				Shoe Pads:		
Therapeutic Treatments:	Special Requirements:			Dates Due:		
Notes (Problems, Consultations, Changes, etc.):				Stable Name / Address:		

CLIENT INFORMATION	Name:	
	Address:	
	Phone:	Email:

HORSE INFORMATION	Name:	Breed:
	Gender:	Primary Use:
	Age:	Temperament (1-10):

Veterinarian:

HOOF ANGLES			HOOF LENGTHS		
	Left	Right		Left	Right
Front			Front		
Back			Back		

Trainer:

Health Concerns:

Supplements:

Shoe Size:

Shoe Type:

Shoe Pads:

Therapeutic Treatments:

Special Requirements:

Dates Due:

Notes (Problems, Consultations, Changes, etc.):

Stable Name / Address:

CLIENT INFORMATION	Name:	
	Address:	
	Phone:	Email:

HORSE INFORMATION	Name:	Breed:
	Gender:	Primary Use:
	Age:	Temperament (1-10):

Veterinarian:

HOOF ANGLES			HOOF LENGTHS		
	Left	Right		Left	Right
Front			Front		
Back			Back		

Trainer:

Health Concerns:

Supplements:

Shoe Size:

Shoe Type:

Shoe Pads:

Therapeutic Treatments:

Special Requirements:

Dates Due:

Notes (Problems, Consultations, Changes, etc.):

Stable Name / Address:

CLIENT INFORMATION	Name:						
	Address:						
	Phone:			Email:			
HORSE INFORMATION	Name:			Breed:			
	Gender:			Primary Use:			
	Age:			Temperament (1-10):			

Veterinarian:	HOOF ANGLES			HOOF LENGTHS		
		Left	Right		Left	Right
Trainer:	Front			Front		
	Back			Back		

Health Concerns:	Supplements:	Shoe Size:
		Shoe Type:
		Shoe Pads:
Therapeutic Treatments:	Special Requirements:	Dates Due:
Notes (Problems, Consultations, Changes, etc.):		Stable Name / Address:

CLIENT INFORMATION	Name:						
	Address:						
	Phone:			Email:			
HORSE INFORMATION	Name:			Breed:			
	Gender:			Primary Use:			
	Age:			Temperament (1-10):			

Veterinarian:	HOOF ANGLES			HOOF LENGTHS		
		Left	Right		Left	Right
Trainer:	Front			Front		
	Back			Back		

Health Concerns:	Supplements:	Shoe Size:
		Shoe Type:
		Shoe Pads:
Therapeutic Treatments:	Special Requirements:	Dates Due:
Notes (Problems, Consultations, Changes, etc.):		Stable Name / Address:

CLIENT INFORMATION	Name:		
	Address:		
	Phone:		Email:

HORSE INFORMATION	Name:	Breed:
	Gender:	Primary Use:
	Age:	Temperament (1-10):

Veterinarian:	HOOF ANGLES			HOOF LENGTHS		
		Left	Right		Left	Right
Trainer:	Front			Front		
	Back			Back		
Health Concerns:	Supplements:			Shoe Size:		
				Shoe Type:		
				Shoe Pads:		
Therapeutic Treatments:	Special Requirements:			Dates Due:		
Notes (Problems, Consultations, Changes, etc.):				Stable Name / Address:		

CLIENT INFORMATION	Name:		
	Address:		
	Phone:		Email:

HORSE INFORMATION	Name:	Breed:
	Gender:	Primary Use:
	Age:	Temperament (1-10):

Veterinarian:	HOOF ANGLES			HOOF LENGTHS		
		Left	Right		Left	Right
Trainer:	Front			Front		
	Back			Back		
Health Concerns:	Supplements:			Shoe Size:		
				Shoe Type:		
				Shoe Pads:		
Therapeutic Treatments:	Special Requirements:			Dates Due:		
Notes (Problems, Consultations, Changes, etc.):				Stable Name / Address:		

CLIENT INFORMATION	Name:	
	Address:	
	Phone:	Email:
HORSE INFORMATION	Name:	Breed:
	Gender:	Primary Use:
	Age:	Temperament (1-10):

Veterinarian:

HOOF ANGLES			HOOF LENGTHS		
	Left	Right		Left	Right
Front			Front		
Back			Back		

Trainer:

Health Concerns:

Supplements:

Shoe Size:

Shoe Type:

Shoe Pads:

Therapeutic Treatments:

Special Requirements:

Dates Due:

Notes (Problems, Consultations, Changes, etc.):

Stable Name / Address:

CLIENT INFORMATION	Name:	
	Address:	
	Phone:	Email:
HORSE INFORMATION	Name:	Breed:
	Gender:	Primary Use:
	Age:	Temperament (1-10):

Veterinarian:

HOOF ANGLES			HOOF LENGTHS		
	Left	Right		Left	Right
Front			Front		
Back			Back		

Trainer:

Health Concerns:

Supplements:

Shoe Size:

Shoe Type:

Shoe Pads:

Therapeutic Treatments:

Special Requirements:

Dates Due:

Notes (Problems, Consultations, Changes, etc.):

Stable Name / Address:

CLIENT INFORMATION	Name:						
	Address:						
	Phone:			Email:			
HORSE INFORMATION	Name:			Breed:			
	Gender:			Primary Use:			
	Age:			Temperament (1-10):			
Veterinarian:	HOOF ANGLES			HOOF LENGTHS			
		Left	Right		Left	Right	
Trainer:	Front			Front			
	Back			Back			
Health Concerns:	Supplements:			Shoe Size:			
				Shoe Type:			
				Shoe Pads:			
Therapeutic Treatments:	Special Requirements:			Dates Due:			
Notes (Problems, Consultations, Changes, etc.):				Stable Name / Address:			

CLIENT INFORMATION	Name:						
	Address:						
	Phone:			Email:			
HORSE INFORMATION	Name:			Breed:			
	Gender:			Primary Use:			
	Age:			Temperament (1-10):			
Veterinarian:	HOOF ANGLES			HOOF LENGTHS			
		Left	Right		Left	Right	
Trainer:	Front			Front			
	Back			Back			
Health Concerns:	Supplements:			Shoe Size:			
				Shoe Type:			
				Shoe Pads:			
Therapeutic Treatments:	Special Requirements:			Dates Due:			
Notes (Problems, Consultations, Changes, etc.):				Stable Name / Address:			

CLIENT INFORMATION	Name:		
	Address:		
	Phone:		Email:

HORSE INFORMATION	Name:	Breed:
	Gender:	Primary Use:
	Age:	Temperament (1-10):

Veterinarian:

HOOF ANGLES		Left	Right
	Front		
	Back		

HOOF LENGTHS		Left	Right
	Front		
	Back		

Trainer:

Health Concerns:

Supplements:

Shoe Size:

Shoe Type:

Shoe Pads:

Therapeutic Treatments:

Special Requirements:

Dates Due:

Notes (Problems, Consultations, Changes, etc.):

Stable Name / Address:

CLIENT INFORMATION	Name:		
	Address:		
	Phone:		Email:

HORSE INFORMATION	Name:	Breed:
	Gender:	Primary Use:
	Age:	Temperament (1-10):

Veterinarian:

HOOF ANGLES		Left	Right
	Front		
	Back		

HOOF LENGTHS		Left	Right
	Front		
	Back		

Trainer:

Health Concerns:

Supplements:

Shoe Size:

Shoe Type:

Shoe Pads:

Therapeutic Treatments:

Special Requirements:

Dates Due:

Notes (Problems, Consultations, Changes, etc.):

Stable Name / Address:

CLIENT INFORMATION	Name:						
	Address:						
	Phone:			Email:			
HORSE INFORMATION	Name:			Breed:			
	Gender:			Primary Use:			
	Age:			Temperament (1-10):			
Veterinarian:	HOOF ANGLES			HOOF LENGTHS			
		Left	Right			Left	Right
Trainer:	Front				Front		
	Back				Back		
Health Concerns:	Supplements:			Shoe Size:			
				Shoe Type:			
				Shoe Pads:			
Therapeutic Treatments:	Special Requirements:			Dates Due:			
Notes (Problems, Consultations, Changes, etc.):				Stable Name / Address:			

CLIENT INFORMATION	Name:						
	Address:						
	Phone:			Email:			
HORSE INFORMATION	Name:			Breed:			
	Gender:			Primary Use:			
	Age:			Temperament (1-10):			
Veterinarian:	HOOF ANGLES			HOOF LENGTHS			
		Left	Right			Left	Right
Trainer:	Front				Front		
	Back				Back		
Health Concerns:	Supplements:			Shoe Size:			
				Shoe Type:			
				Shoe Pads:			
Therapeutic Treatments:	Special Requirements:			Dates Due:			
Notes (Problems, Consultations, Changes, etc.):				Stable Name / Address:			

CLIENT INFORMATION	Name:						
	Address:						
	Phone:				Email:		
HORSE INFORMATION	Name:				Breed:		
	Gender:				Primary Use:		
	Age:				Temperament (1-10):		

Veterinarian:	HOOF ANGLES			HOOF LENGTHS		
		Left	Right		Left	Right
Trainer:	Front			Front		
	Back			Back		

Health Concerns:	Supplements:	Shoe Size:
		Shoe Type:
		Shoe Pads:
Therapeutic Treatments:	Special Requirements:	Dates Due:
Notes (Problems, Consultations, Changes, etc.):		Stable Name / Address:

CLIENT INFORMATION	Name:						
	Address:						
	Phone:				Email:		
HORSE INFORMATION	Name:				Breed:		
	Gender:				Primary Use:		
	Age:				Temperament (1-10):		

Veterinarian:	HOOF ANGLES			HOOF LENGTHS		
		Left	Right		Left	Right
Trainer:	Front			Front		
	Back			Back		

Health Concerns:	Supplements:	Shoe Size:
		Shoe Type:
		Shoe Pads:
Therapeutic Treatments:	Special Requirements:	Dates Due:
Notes (Problems, Consultations, Changes, etc.):		Stable Name / Address:

CLIENT INFORMATION	Name:						
	Address:						
	Phone:			Email:			
HORSE INFORMATION	Name:			Breed:			
	Gender:			Primary Use:			
	Age:			Temperament (1-10):			

Veterinarian:	HOOF ANGLES			HOOF LENGTHS		
		Left	Right		Left	Right
Trainer:	Front			Front		
	Back			Back		
Health Concerns:	Supplements:			Shoe Size:		
				Shoe Type:		
				Shoe Pads:		
Therapeutic Treatments:	Special Requirements:			Dates Due:		
Notes (Problems, Consultations, Changes, etc.):				Stable Name / Address:		

CLIENT INFORMATION	Name:						
	Address:						
	Phone:			Email:			
HORSE INFORMATION	Name:			Breed:			
	Gender:			Primary Use:			
	Age:			Temperament (1-10):			

Veterinarian:	HOOF ANGLES			HOOF LENGTHS		
		Left	Right		Left	Right
Trainer:	Front			Front		
	Back			Back		
Health Concerns:	Supplements:			Shoe Size:		
				Shoe Type:		
				Shoe Pads:		
Therapeutic Treatments:	Special Requirements:			Dates Due:		
Notes (Problems, Consultations, Changes, etc.):				Stable Name / Address:		

Form 1

CLIENT INFORMATION	Name:	
	Address:	
	Phone:	Email:

HORSE INFORMATION	Name:	Breed:
	Gender:	Primary Use:
	Age:	Temperament (1-10):

Veterinarian:	HOOF ANGLES			HOOF LENGTHS		
		Left	Right		Left	Right
Trainer:	Front			Front		
	Back			Back		
Health Concerns:	Supplements:			Shoe Size:		
				Shoe Type:		
				Shoe Pads:		
Therapeutic Treatments:	Special Requirements:			Dates Due:		
Notes (Problems, Consultations, Changes, etc.):				Stable Name / Address:		

Form 2

CLIENT INFORMATION	Name:	
	Address:	
	Phone:	Email:

HORSE INFORMATION	Name:	Breed:
	Gender:	Primary Use:
	Age:	Temperament (1-10):

Veterinarian:	HOOF ANGLES			HOOF LENGTHS		
		Left	Right		Left	Right
Trainer:	Front			Front		
	Back			Back		
Health Concerns:	Supplements:			Shoe Size:		
				Shoe Type:		
				Shoe Pads:		
Therapeutic Treatments:	Special Requirements:			Dates Due:		
Notes (Problems, Consultations, Changes, etc.):				Stable Name / Address:		

CLIENT INFORMATION	Name:		
	Address:		
	Phone:		Email:
HORSE INFORMATION	Name:		Breed:
	Gender:		Primary Use:
	Age:		Temperament (1-10):

Veterinarian:	HOOF ANGLES			HOOF LENGTHS		
		Left	Right		Left	Right
Trainer:	Front			Front		
	Back			Back		
Health Concerns:	Supplements:			Shoe Size:		
				Shoe Type:		
				Shoe Pads:		
Therapeutic Treatments:	Special Requirements:			Dates Due:		
Notes (Problems, Consultations, Changes, etc.):				Stable Name / Address:		

CLIENT INFORMATION	Name:		
	Address:		
	Phone:		Email:
HORSE INFORMATION	Name:		Breed:
	Gender:		Primary Use:
	Age:		Temperament (1-10):

Veterinarian:	HOOF ANGLES			HOOF LENGTHS		
		Left	Right		Left	Right
Trainer:	Front			Front		
	Back			Back		
Health Concerns:	Supplements:			Shoe Size:		
				Shoe Type:		
				Shoe Pads:		
Therapeutic Treatments:	Special Requirements:			Dates Due:		
Notes (Problems, Consultations, Changes, etc.):				Stable Name / Address:		

CLIENT INFORMATION	Name:		
	Address:		
	Phone:		Email:
HORSE INFORMATION	Name:		Breed:
	Gender:		Primary Use:
	Age:		Temperament (1-10):

Veterinarian:	HOOF ANGLES			HOOF LENGTHS		
		Left	Right		Left	Right
Trainer:	Front			Front		
	Back			Back		
Health Concerns:	Supplements:			Shoe Size:		
				Shoe Type:		
				Shoe Pads:		
Therapeutic Treatments:	Special Requirements:			Dates Due:		
Notes (Problems, Consultations, Changes, etc.):				Stable Name / Address:		

CLIENT INFORMATION	Name:		
	Address:		
	Phone:		Email:
HORSE INFORMATION	Name:		Breed:
	Gender:		Primary Use:
	Age:		Temperament (1-10):

Veterinarian:	HOOF ANGLES			HOOF LENGTHS		
		Left	Right		Left	Right
Trainer:	Front			Front		
	Back			Back		
Health Concerns:	Supplements:			Shoe Size:		
				Shoe Type:		
				Shoe Pads:		
Therapeutic Treatments:	Special Requirements:			Dates Due:		
Notes (Problems, Consultations, Changes, etc.):				Stable Name / Address:		

CLIENT INFORMATION	Name:						
	Address:						
	Phone:			Email:			
HORSE INFORMATION	Name:			Breed:			
	Gender:			Primary Use:			
	Age:			Temperament (1-10):			

Veterinarian:	HOOF ANGLES			HOOF LENGTHS		
		Left	Right		Left	Right
Trainer:	Front			Front		
	Back			Back		
Health Concerns:	Supplements:			Shoe Size:		
				Shoe Type:		
				Shoe Pads:		
Therapeutic Treatments:	Special Requirements:			Dates Due:		
Notes (Problems, Consultations, Changes, etc.):				Stable Name / Address:		

CLIENT INFORMATION	Name:						
	Address:						
	Phone:			Email:			
HORSE INFORMATION	Name:			Breed:			
	Gender:			Primary Use:			
	Age:			Temperament (1-10):			

Veterinarian:	HOOF ANGLES			HOOF LENGTHS		
		Left	Right		Left	Right
Trainer:	Front			Front		
	Back			Back		
Health Concerns:	Supplements:			Shoe Size:		
				Shoe Type:		
				Shoe Pads:		
Therapeutic Treatments:	Special Requirements:			Dates Due:		
Notes (Problems, Consultations, Changes, etc.):				Stable Name / Address:		

CLIENT INFORMATION	Name:						
	Address:						
	Phone:			Email:			

HORSE INFORMATION	Name:			Breed:			
	Gender:			Primary Use:			
	Age:			Temperament (1-10):			

Veterinarian:	HOOF ANGLES			HOOF LENGTHS		
		Left	Right		Left	Right
Trainer:	Front			Front		
	Back			Back		
Health Concerns:	Supplements:			Shoe Size:		
				Shoe Type:		
				Shoe Pads:		
Therapeutic Treatments:	Special Requirements:			Dates Due:		
Notes (Problems, Consultations, Changes, etc.):				Stable Name / Address:		

CLIENT INFORMATION	Name:						
	Address:						
	Phone:			Email:			

HORSE INFORMATION	Name:			Breed:			
	Gender:			Primary Use:			
	Age:			Temperament (1-10):			

Veterinarian:	HOOF ANGLES			HOOF LENGTHS		
		Left	Right		Left	Right
Trainer:	Front			Front		
	Back			Back		
Health Concerns:	Supplements:			Shoe Size:		
				Shoe Type:		
				Shoe Pads:		
Therapeutic Treatments:	Special Requirements:			Dates Due:		
Notes (Problems, Consultations, Changes, etc.):				Stable Name / Address:		

CLIENT INFORMATION	Name:		
	Address:		
	Phone:		Email:

HORSE INFORMATION	Name:		Breed:
	Gender:		Primary Use:
	Age:		Temperament (1-10):

Veterinarian:	HOOF ANGLES			HOOF LENGTHS		
		Left	Right		Left	Right
Trainer:	Front			Front		
	Back			Back		

Health Concerns:	Supplements:	Shoe Size:
		Shoe Type:
		Shoe Pads:

| Therapeutic Treatments: | Special Requirements: | Dates Due: |

| Notes (Problems, Consultations, Changes, etc.): | Stable Name / Address: |

CLIENT INFORMATION	Name:		
	Address:		
	Phone:		Email:

HORSE INFORMATION	Name:		Breed:
	Gender:		Primary Use:
	Age:		Temperament (1-10):

Veterinarian:	HOOF ANGLES			HOOF LENGTHS		
		Left	Right		Left	Right
Trainer:	Front			Front		
	Back			Back		

Health Concerns:	Supplements:	Shoe Size:
		Shoe Type:
		Shoe Pads:

| Therapeutic Treatments: | Special Requirements: | Dates Due: |

| Notes (Problems, Consultations, Changes, etc.): | Stable Name / Address: |

CLIENT INFORMATION	Name:						
	Address:						
	Phone:			Email:			
HORSE INFORMATION	Name:			Breed:			
	Gender:			Primary Use:			
	Age:			Temperament (1-10):			

Veterinarian:	HOOF ANGLES			HOOF LENGTHS		
		Left	Right		Left	Right
Trainer:	Front			Front		
	Back			Back		

Health Concerns:	Supplements:	Shoe Size:
		Shoe Type:
		Shoe Pads:
Therapeutic Treatments:	Special Requirements:	Dates Due:
Notes (Problems, Consultations, Changes, etc.):		Stable Name / Address:

CLIENT INFORMATION	Name:						
	Address:						
	Phone:			Email:			
HORSE INFORMATION	Name:			Breed:			
	Gender:			Primary Use:			
	Age:			Temperament (1-10):			

Veterinarian:	HOOF ANGLES			HOOF LENGTHS		
		Left	Right		Left	Right
Trainer:	Front			Front		
	Back			Back		

Health Concerns:	Supplements:	Shoe Size:
		Shoe Type:
		Shoe Pads:
Therapeutic Treatments:	Special Requirements:	Dates Due:
Notes (Problems, Consultations, Changes, etc.):		Stable Name / Address:

CLIENT INFORMATION	Name:						
	Address:						
	Phone:			Email:			
HORSE INFORMATION	Name:			Breed:			
	Gender:			Primary Use:			
	Age:			Temperament (1-10):			

Veterinarian:	HOOF ANGLES			HOOF LENGTHS		
		Left	Right		Left	Right
Trainer:	Front			Front		
	Back			Back		
Health Concerns:	Supplements:			Shoe Size:		
				Shoe Type:		
				Shoe Pads:		
Therapeutic Treatments:	Special Requirements:			Dates Due:		
Notes (Problems, Consultations, Changes, etc.):				Stable Name / Address:		

CLIENT INFORMATION	Name:						
	Address:						
	Phone:			Email:			
HORSE INFORMATION	Name:			Breed:			
	Gender:			Primary Use:			
	Age:			Temperament (1-10):			

Veterinarian:	HOOF ANGLES			HOOF LENGTHS		
		Left	Right		Left	Right
Trainer:	Front			Front		
	Back			Back		
Health Concerns:	Supplements:			Shoe Size:		
				Shoe Type:		
				Shoe Pads:		
Therapeutic Treatments:	Special Requirements:			Dates Due:		
Notes (Problems, Consultations, Changes, etc.):				Stable Name / Address:		

CLIENT INFORMATION	Name:		
	Address:		
	Phone:		Email:
HORSE INFORMATION	Name:		Breed:
	Gender:		Primary Use:
	Age:		Temperament (1-10):

Veterinarian:	HOOF ANGLES			HOOF LENGTHS		
		Left	Right		Left	Right
Trainer:	Front			Front		
	Back			Back		

Health Concerns:	Supplements:	Shoe Size:
		Shoe Type:
		Shoe Pads:
Therapeutic Treatments:	Special Requirements:	Dates Due:

Notes (Problems, Consultations, Changes, etc.):	Stable Name / Address:

CLIENT INFORMATION	Name:		
	Address:		
	Phone:		Email:
HORSE INFORMATION	Name:		Breed:
	Gender:		Primary Use:
	Age:		Temperament (1-10):

Veterinarian:	HOOF ANGLES			HOOF LENGTHS		
		Left	Right		Left	Right
Trainer:	Front			Front		
	Back			Back		

Health Concerns:	Supplements:	Shoe Size:
		Shoe Type:
		Shoe Pads:
Therapeutic Treatments:	Special Requirements:	Dates Due:

Notes (Problems, Consultations, Changes, etc.):	Stable Name / Address:

CLIENT INFORMATION	Name:						
	Address:						
	Phone:				Email:		
HORSE INFORMATION	Name:				Breed:		
	Gender:				Primary Use:		
	Age:				Temperament (1-10):		

Veterinarian:	HOOF ANGLES			HOOF LENGTHS		
		Left	Right		Left	Right
Trainer:	Front			Front		
	Back			Back		
Health Concerns:	Supplements:			Shoe Size:		
				Shoe Type:		
				Shoe Pads:		
Therapeutic Treatments:	Special Requirements:			Dates Due:		
Notes (Problems, Consultations, Changes, etc.):				Stable Name / Address:		

CLIENT INFORMATION	Name:						
	Address:						
	Phone:				Email:		
HORSE INFORMATION	Name:				Breed:		
	Gender:				Primary Use:		
	Age:				Temperament (1-10):		

Veterinarian:	HOOF ANGLES			HOOF LENGTHS		
		Left	Right		Left	Right
Trainer:	Front			Front		
	Back			Back		
Health Concerns:	Supplements:			Shoe Size:		
				Shoe Type:		
				Shoe Pads:		
Therapeutic Treatments:	Special Requirements:			Dates Due:		
Notes (Problems, Consultations, Changes, etc.):				Stable Name / Address:		

CLIENT INFORMATION	Name:		
	Address:		
	Phone:		Email:
HORSE INFORMATION	Name:		Breed:
	Gender:		Primary Use:
	Age:		Temperament (1-10):

Veterinarian:	HOOF ANGLES			HOOF LENGTHS		
		Left	Right		Left	Right
Trainer:	Front			Front		
	Back			Back		
Health Concerns:	Supplements:			Shoe Size:		
				Shoe Type:		
				Shoe Pads:		
Therapeutic Treatments:	Special Requirements:			Dates Due:		
Notes (Problems, Consultations, Changes, etc.):				Stable Name / Address:		

CLIENT INFORMATION	Name:		
	Address:		
	Phone:		Email:
HORSE INFORMATION	Name:		Breed:
	Gender:		Primary Use:
	Age:		Temperament (1-10):

Veterinarian:	HOOF ANGLES			HOOF LENGTHS		
		Left	Right		Left	Right
Trainer:	Front			Front		
	Back			Back		
Health Concerns:	Supplements:			Shoe Size:		
				Shoe Type:		
				Shoe Pads:		
Therapeutic Treatments:	Special Requirements:			Dates Due:		
Notes (Problems, Consultations, Changes, etc.):				Stable Name / Address:		

CLIENT INFORMATION	Name:						
	Address:						
	Phone:				Email:		
HORSE INFORMATION	Name:				Breed:		
	Gender:				Primary Use:		
	Age:				Temperament (1-10):		

Veterinarian:	HOOF ANGLES			HOOF LENGTHS		
		Left	Right		Left	Right
Trainer:	Front			Front		
	Back			Back		

Health Concerns:	Supplements:	Shoe Size:
		Shoe Type:
		Shoe Pads:
Therapeutic Treatments:	Special Requirements:	Dates Due:
Notes (Problems, Consultations, Changes, etc.):		Stable Name / Address:

CLIENT INFORMATION	Name:						
	Address:						
	Phone:				Email:		
HORSE INFORMATION	Name:				Breed:		
	Gender:				Primary Use:		
	Age:				Temperament (1-10):		

Veterinarian:	HOOF ANGLES			HOOF LENGTHS		
		Left	Right		Left	Right
Trainer:	Front			Front		
	Back			Back		

Health Concerns:	Supplements:	Shoe Size:
		Shoe Type:
		Shoe Pads:
Therapeutic Treatments:	Special Requirements:	Dates Due:
Notes (Problems, Consultations, Changes, etc.):		Stable Name / Address:

Form 1

CLIENT INFORMATION	Name:	
	Address:	
	Phone:	Email:

HORSE INFORMATION	Name:	Breed:
	Gender:	Primary Use:
	Age:	Temperament (1-10):

Veterinarian:	HOOF ANGLES			HOOF LENGTHS		
		Left	Right		Left	Right
Trainer:	Front			Front		
	Back			Back		

Health Concerns:	Supplements:	Shoe Size:
		Shoe Type:
		Shoe Pads:
Therapeutic Treatments:	Special Requirements:	Dates Due:

Notes (Problems, Consultations, Changes, etc.):	Stable Name / Address:

Form 2

CLIENT INFORMATION	Name:	
	Address:	
	Phone:	Email:

HORSE INFORMATION	Name:	Breed:
	Gender:	Primary Use:
	Age:	Temperament (1-10):

Veterinarian:	HOOF ANGLES			HOOF LENGTHS		
		Left	Right		Left	Right
Trainer:	Front			Front		
	Back			Back		

Health Concerns:	Supplements:	Shoe Size:
		Shoe Type:
		Shoe Pads:
Therapeutic Treatments:	Special Requirements:	Dates Due:

Notes (Problems, Consultations, Changes, etc.):	Stable Name / Address:

CLIENT INFORMATION	Name:		
	Address:		
	Phone:	Email:	

HORSE INFORMATION	Name:	Breed:	
	Gender:	Primary Use:	
	Age:	Temperament (1-10):	

Veterinarian:	HOOF ANGLES			HOOF LENGTHS		
		Left	Right		Left	Right
Trainer:	Front			Front		
	Back			Back		

Health Concerns:	Supplements:		Shoe Size:
			Shoe Type:
			Shoe Pads:
Therapeutic Treatments:	Special Requirements:		Dates Due:

| Notes (Problems, Consultations, Changes, etc.): | | Stable Name / Address: |

CLIENT INFORMATION	Name:		
	Address:		
	Phone:	Email:	

HORSE INFORMATION	Name:	Breed:	
	Gender:	Primary Use:	
	Age:	Temperament (1-10):	

Veterinarian:	HOOF ANGLES			HOOF LENGTHS		
		Left	Right		Left	Right
Trainer:	Front			Front		
	Back			Back		

Health Concerns:	Supplements:		Shoe Size:
			Shoe Type:
			Shoe Pads:
Therapeutic Treatments:	Special Requirements:		Dates Due:

| Notes (Problems, Consultations, Changes, etc.): | | Stable Name / Address: |

CLIENT INFORMATION	Name:	
	Address:	
	Phone:	Email:

HORSE INFORMATION	Name:	Breed:
	Gender:	Primary Use:
	Age:	Temperament (1-10):

Veterinarian:	HOOF ANGLES			HOOF LENGTHS		
		Left	Right		Left	Right
Trainer:	Front			Front		
	Back			Back		
Health Concerns:	Supplements:			Shoe Size:		
				Shoe Type:		
				Shoe Pads:		
Therapeutic Treatments:	Special Requirements:			Dates Due:		
Notes (Problems, Consultations, Changes, etc.):				Stable Name / Address:		

CLIENT INFORMATION	Name:	
	Address:	
	Phone:	Email:

HORSE INFORMATION	Name:	Breed:
	Gender:	Primary Use:
	Age:	Temperament (1-10):

Veterinarian:	HOOF ANGLES			HOOF LENGTHS		
		Left	Right		Left	Right
Trainer:	Front			Front		
	Back			Back		
Health Concerns:	Supplements:			Shoe Size:		
				Shoe Type:		
				Shoe Pads:		
Therapeutic Treatments:	Special Requirements:			Dates Due:		
Notes (Problems, Consultations, Changes, etc.):				Stable Name / Address:		

CLIENT INFORMATION	Name:		
	Address:		
	Phone:		Email:
HORSE INFORMATION	Name:		Breed:
	Gender:		Primary Use:
	Age:		Temperament (1-10):

Veterinarian:	HOOF ANGLES			HOOF LENGTHS		
		Left	Right		Left	Right
Trainer:	Front			Front		
	Back			Back		
Health Concerns:	Supplements:		Shoe Size:
			Shoe Type:
			Shoe Pads:
Therapeutic Treatments:	Special Requirements:		Dates Due:
Notes (Problems, Consultations, Changes, etc.):			Stable Name / Address:

CLIENT INFORMATION	Name:		
	Address:		
	Phone:		Email:
HORSE INFORMATION	Name:		Breed:
	Gender:		Primary Use:
	Age:		Temperament (1-10):

Veterinarian:	HOOF ANGLES			HOOF LENGTHS		
		Left	Right		Left	Right
Trainer:	Front			Front		
	Back			Back		
Health Concerns:	Supplements:		Shoe Size:
			Shoe Type:
			Shoe Pads:
Therapeutic Treatments:	Special Requirements:		Dates Due:
Notes (Problems, Consultations, Changes, etc.):			Stable Name / Address:

CLIENT INFORMATION	Name:							
	Address:							
	Phone:				Email:			
HORSE INFORMATION	Name:				Breed:			
	Gender:				Primary Use:			
	Age:				Temperament (1-10):			

Veterinarian:	HOOF ANGLES			HOOF LENGTHS		
		Left	Right		Left	Right
Trainer:	Front			Front		
	Back			Back		
Health Concerns:	Supplements:			Shoe Size:		
				Shoe Type:		
				Shoe Pads:		
Therapeutic Treatments:	Special Requirements:			Dates Due:		
Notes (Problems, Consultations, Changes, etc.):				Stable Name / Address:		

CLIENT INFORMATION	Name:							
	Address:							
	Phone:				Email:			
HORSE INFORMATION	Name:				Breed:			
	Gender:				Primary Use:			
	Age:				Temperament (1-10):			

Veterinarian:	HOOF ANGLES			HOOF LENGTHS		
		Left	Right		Left	Right
Trainer:	Front			Front		
	Back			Back		
Health Concerns:	Supplements:			Shoe Size:		
				Shoe Type:		
				Shoe Pads:		
Therapeutic Treatments:	Special Requirements:			Dates Due:		
Notes (Problems, Consultations, Changes, etc.):				Stable Name / Address:		

CLIENT INFORMATION	Name:	
	Address:	
	Phone:	Email:

HORSE INFORMATION	Name:	Breed:
	Gender:	Primary Use:
	Age:	Temperament (1-10):

Veterinarian:	HOOF ANGLES			HOOF LENGTHS		
		Left	Right		Left	Right
Trainer:	Front			Front		
	Back			Back		
Health Concerns:	Supplements:			Shoe Size:		
				Shoe Type:		
				Shoe Pads:		
Therapeutic Treatments:	Special Requirements:			Dates Due:		
Notes (Problems, Consultations, Changes, etc.):				Stable Name / Address:		

CLIENT INFORMATION	Name:	
	Address:	
	Phone:	Email:

HORSE INFORMATION	Name:	Breed:
	Gender:	Primary Use:
	Age:	Temperament (1-10):

Veterinarian:	HOOF ANGLES			HOOF LENGTHS		
		Left	Right		Left	Right
Trainer:	Front			Front		
	Back			Back		
Health Concerns:	Supplements:			Shoe Size:		
				Shoe Type:		
				Shoe Pads:		
Therapeutic Treatments:	Special Requirements:			Dates Due:		
Notes (Problems, Consultations, Changes, etc.):				Stable Name / Address:		

CLIENT INFORMATION	Name:						
	Address:						
	Phone:			Email:			
HORSE INFORMATION	Name:			Breed:			
	Gender:			Primary Use:			
	Age:			Temperament (1-10):			

Veterinarian:	HOOF ANGLES			HOOF LENGTHS		
		Left	Right		Left	Right
Trainer:	Front			Front		
	Back			Back		
Health Concerns:	Supplements:			Shoe Size:		
				Shoe Type:		
				Shoe Pads:		
Therapeutic Treatments:	Special Requirements:			Dates Due:		
Notes (Problems, Consultations, Changes, etc.):				Stable Name / Address:		

CLIENT INFORMATION	Name:						
	Address:						
	Phone:			Email:			
HORSE INFORMATION	Name:			Breed:			
	Gender:			Primary Use:			
	Age:			Temperament (1-10):			

Veterinarian:	HOOF ANGLES			HOOF LENGTHS		
		Left	Right		Left	Right
Trainer:	Front			Front		
	Back			Back		
Health Concerns:	Supplements:			Shoe Size:		
				Shoe Type:		
				Shoe Pads:		
Therapeutic Treatments:	Special Requirements:			Dates Due:		
Notes (Problems, Consultations, Changes, etc.):				Stable Name / Address:		

CLIENT INFORMATION	Name:	
	Address:	
	Phone:	Email:

HORSE INFORMATION	Name:	Breed:
	Gender:	Primary Use:
	Age:	Temperament (1-10):

Veterinarian:	HOOF ANGLES			HOOF LENGTHS		
		Left	Right		Left	Right
Trainer:	Front			Front		
	Back			Back		

Health Concerns:	Supplements:		Shoe Size:
			Shoe Type:
			Shoe Pads:
Therapeutic Treatments:	Special Requirements:		Dates Due:

| Notes (Problems, Consultations, Changes, etc.): | Stable Name / Address: |

CLIENT INFORMATION	Name:	
	Address:	
	Phone:	Email:

HORSE INFORMATION	Name:	Breed:
	Gender:	Primary Use:
	Age:	Temperament (1-10):

Veterinarian:	HOOF ANGLES			HOOF LENGTHS		
		Left	Right		Left	Right
Trainer:	Front			Front		
	Back			Back		

Health Concerns:	Supplements:		Shoe Size:
			Shoe Type:
			Shoe Pads:
Therapeutic Treatments:	Special Requirements:		Dates Due:

| Notes (Problems, Consultations, Changes, etc.): | Stable Name / Address: |

CLIENT INFORMATION	Name:						
	Address:						
	Phone:				Email:		
HORSE INFORMATION	Name:				Breed:		
	Gender:				Primary Use:		
	Age:				Temperament (1-10):		

Veterinarian:	HOOF ANGLES			HOOF LENGTHS		
		Left	Right		Left	Right
Trainer:	Front			Front		
	Back			Back		

Health Concerns:	Supplements:	Shoe Size:
		Shoe Type:
		Shoe Pads:
Therapeutic Treatments:	Special Requirements:	Dates Due:
Notes (Problems, Consultations, Changes, etc.):		Stable Name / Address:

CLIENT INFORMATION	Name:						
	Address:						
	Phone:				Email:		
HORSE INFORMATION	Name:				Breed:		
	Gender:				Primary Use:		
	Age:				Temperament (1-10):		

Veterinarian:	HOOF ANGLES			HOOF LENGTHS		
		Left	Right		Left	Right
Trainer:	Front			Front		
	Back			Back		

Health Concerns:	Supplements:	Shoe Size:
		Shoe Type:
		Shoe Pads:
Therapeutic Treatments:	Special Requirements:	Dates Due:
Notes (Problems, Consultations, Changes, etc.):		Stable Name / Address:

CLIENT INFORMATION	Name:			
	Address:			
	Phone:		Email:	

HORSE INFORMATION	Name:		Breed:	
	Gender:		Primary Use:	
	Age:		Temperament (1-10):	

Veterinarian:	HOOF ANGLES			HOOF LENGTHS		
		Left	Right		Left	Right
Trainer:	Front			Front		
	Back			Back		

Health Concerns:	Supplements:	Shoe Size:
		Shoe Type:
		Shoe Pads:
Therapeutic Treatments:	Special Requirements:	Dates Due:

| Notes (Problems, Consultations, Changes, etc.): | Stable Name / Address: |

CLIENT INFORMATION	Name:			
	Address:			
	Phone:		Email:	

HORSE INFORMATION	Name:		Breed:	
	Gender:		Primary Use:	
	Age:		Temperament (1-10):	

Veterinarian:	HOOF ANGLES			HOOF LENGTHS		
		Left	Right		Left	Right
Trainer:	Front			Front		
	Back			Back		

Health Concerns:	Supplements:	Shoe Size:
		Shoe Type:
		Shoe Pads:
Therapeutic Treatments:	Special Requirements:	Dates Due:

| Notes (Problems, Consultations, Changes, etc.): | Stable Name / Address: |

CLIENT INFORMATION	Name:		
	Address:		
	Phone:		Email:

HORSE INFORMATION	Name:		Breed:
	Gender:		Primary Use:
	Age:		Temperament (1-10):

Veterinarian:	HOOF ANGLES			HOOF LENGTHS		
		Left	Right		Left	Right
Trainer:	Front			Front		
	Back			Back		

Health Concerns:	Supplements:	Shoe Size:
		Shoe Type:
		Shoe Pads:
Therapeutic Treatments:	Special Requirements:	Dates Due:

| Notes (Problems, Consultations, Changes, etc.): | Stable Name / Address: |

CLIENT INFORMATION	Name:		
	Address:		
	Phone:		Email:

HORSE INFORMATION	Name:		Breed:
	Gender:		Primary Use:
	Age:		Temperament (1-10):

Veterinarian:	HOOF ANGLES			HOOF LENGTHS		
		Left	Right		Left	Right
Trainer:	Front			Front		
	Back			Back		

Health Concerns:	Supplements:	Shoe Size:
		Shoe Type:
		Shoe Pads:
Therapeutic Treatments:	Special Requirements:	Dates Due:

| Notes (Problems, Consultations, Changes, etc.): | Stable Name / Address: |

CLIENT INFORMATION	Name:		
	Address:		
	Phone:		Email:
HORSE INFORMATION	Name:		Breed:
	Gender:		Primary Use:
	Age:		Temperament (1-10):

Veterinarian:	HOOF ANGLES			HOOF LENGTHS		
		Left	Right		Left	Right
Trainer:	Front			Front		
	Back			Back		

Health Concerns:	Supplements:	Shoe Size:
		Shoe Type:
		Shoe Pads:
Therapeutic Treatments:	Special Requirements:	Dates Due:
Notes (Problems, Consultations, Changes, etc.):		Stable Name / Address:

CLIENT INFORMATION	Name:		
	Address:		
	Phone:		Email:
HORSE INFORMATION	Name:		Breed:
	Gender:		Primary Use:
	Age:		Temperament (1-10):

Veterinarian:	HOOF ANGLES			HOOF LENGTHS		
		Left	Right		Left	Right
Trainer:	Front			Front		
	Back			Back		

Health Concerns:	Supplements:	Shoe Size:
		Shoe Type:
		Shoe Pads:
Therapeutic Treatments:	Special Requirements:	Dates Due:
Notes (Problems, Consultations, Changes, etc.):		Stable Name / Address:

CLIENT INFORMATION	Name:		
	Address:		
	Phone:		Email:

HORSE INFORMATION	Name:		Breed:
	Gender:		Primary Use:
	Age:		Temperament (1-10):

Veterinarian:	HOOF ANGLES			HOOF LENGTHS		
		Left	Right		Left	Right
Trainer:	Front			Front		
	Back			Back		

Health Concerns:	Supplements:	Shoe Size:
		Shoe Type:
		Shoe Pads:
Therapeutic Treatments:	Special Requirements:	Dates Due:
Notes (Problems, Consultations, Changes, etc.):		Stable Name / Address:

CLIENT INFORMATION	Name:		
	Address:		
	Phone:		Email:

HORSE INFORMATION	Name:		Breed:
	Gender:		Primary Use:
	Age:		Temperament (1-10):

Veterinarian:	HOOF ANGLES			HOOF LENGTHS		
		Left	Right		Left	Right
Trainer:	Front			Front		
	Back			Back		

Health Concerns:	Supplements:	Shoe Size:
		Shoe Type:
		Shoe Pads:
Therapeutic Treatments:	Special Requirements:	Dates Due:
Notes (Problems, Consultations, Changes, etc.):		Stable Name / Address:

CLIENT INFORMATION	Name:	
	Address:	
	Phone:	Email:
HORSE INFORMATION	Name:	Breed:
	Gender:	Primary Use:
	Age:	Temperament (1-10):

Veterinarian:	HOOF ANGLES			HOOF LENGTHS		
		Left	Right		Left	Right
Trainer:	Front			Front		
	Back			Back		
Health Concerns:	Supplements:			Shoe Size:		
				Shoe Type:		
				Shoe Pads:		
Therapeutic Treatments:	Special Requirements:			Dates Due:		
Notes (Problems, Consultations, Changes, etc.):				Stable Name / Address:		

CLIENT INFORMATION	Name:	
	Address:	
	Phone:	Email:
HORSE INFORMATION	Name:	Breed:
	Gender:	Primary Use:
	Age:	Temperament (1-10):

Veterinarian:	HOOF ANGLES			HOOF LENGTHS		
		Left	Right		Left	Right
Trainer:	Front			Front		
	Back			Back		
Health Concerns:	Supplements:			Shoe Size:		
				Shoe Type:		
				Shoe Pads:		
Therapeutic Treatments:	Special Requirements:			Dates Due:		
Notes (Problems, Consultations, Changes, etc.):				Stable Name / Address:		

Form 1

CLIENT INFORMATION	Name:	
	Address:	
	Phone:	Email:

HORSE INFORMATION	Name:	Breed:
	Gender:	Primary Use:
	Age:	Temperament (1-10):

Veterinarian:

HOOF ANGLES			HOOF LENGTHS		
	Left	Right		Left	Right
Front			Front		
Back			Back		

Trainer:

Health Concerns:

Supplements:	Shoe Size:
	Shoe Type:
	Shoe Pads:

Therapeutic Treatments:

Special Requirements:	Dates Due:

Notes (Problems, Consultations, Changes, etc.):	Stable Name / Address:

Form 2

CLIENT INFORMATION	Name:	
	Address:	
	Phone:	Email:

HORSE INFORMATION	Name:	Breed:
	Gender:	Primary Use:
	Age:	Temperament (1-10):

Veterinarian:

HOOF ANGLES			HOOF LENGTHS		
	Left	Right		Left	Right
Front			Front		
Back			Back		

Trainer:

Health Concerns:

Supplements:	Shoe Size:
	Shoe Type:
	Shoe Pads:

Therapeutic Treatments:

Special Requirements:	Dates Due:

Notes (Problems, Consultations, Changes, etc.):	Stable Name / Address:

Form 1

CLIENT INFORMATION	Name:	
	Address:	
	Phone:	Email:

HORSE INFORMATION	Name:	Breed:
	Gender:	Primary Use:
	Age:	Temperament (1-10):

Veterinarian:	HOOF ANGLES			HOOF LENGTHS		
		Left	Right		Left	Right
Trainer:	Front			Front		
	Back			Back		

Health Concerns:	Supplements:	Shoe Size:
		Shoe Type:
		Shoe Pads:
Therapeutic Treatments:	Special Requirements:	Dates Due:

Notes (Problems, Consultations, Changes, etc.):	Stable Name / Address:

Form 2

CLIENT INFORMATION	Name:	
	Address:	
	Phone:	Email:

HORSE INFORMATION	Name:	Breed:
	Gender:	Primary Use:
	Age:	Temperament (1-10):

Veterinarian:	HOOF ANGLES			HOOF LENGTHS		
		Left	Right		Left	Right
Trainer:	Front			Front		
	Back			Back		

Health Concerns:	Supplements:	Shoe Size:
		Shoe Type:
		Shoe Pads:
Therapeutic Treatments:	Special Requirements:	Dates Due:

Notes (Problems, Consultations, Changes, etc.):	Stable Name / Address:

CLIENT INFORMATION	Name:						
	Address:						
	Phone:			Email:			
HORSE INFORMATION	Name:			Breed:			
	Gender:			Primary Use:			
	Age:			Temperament (1-10):			

Veterinarian:	HOOF ANGLES			HOOF LENGTHS		
		Left	Right		Left	Right
Trainer:	Front			Front		
	Back			Back		
Health Concerns:	Supplements:			Shoe Size:		
				Shoe Type:		
				Shoe Pads:		
Therapeutic Treatments:	Special Requirements:			Dates Due:		
Notes (Problems, Consultations, Changes, etc.):				Stable Name / Address:		

CLIENT INFORMATION	Name:						
	Address:						
	Phone:			Email:			
HORSE INFORMATION	Name:			Breed:			
	Gender:			Primary Use:			
	Age:			Temperament (1-10):			

Veterinarian:	HOOF ANGLES			HOOF LENGTHS		
		Left	Right		Left	Right
Trainer:	Front			Front		
	Back			Back		
Health Concerns:	Supplements:			Shoe Size:		
				Shoe Type:		
				Shoe Pads:		
Therapeutic Treatments:	Special Requirements:			Dates Due:		
Notes (Problems, Consultations, Changes, etc.):				Stable Name / Address:		

CLIENT INFORMATION	Name:	
	Address:	
	Phone:	Email:

HORSE INFORMATION	Name:	Breed:
	Gender:	Primary Use:
	Age:	Temperament (1-10):

Veterinarian:	HOOF ANGLES			HOOF LENGTHS		
		Left	Right		Left	Right
Trainer:	Front			Front		
	Back			Back		
Health Concerns:	Supplements:			Shoe Size:		
				Shoe Type:		
				Shoe Pads:		
Therapeutic Treatments:	Special Requirements:			Dates Due:		
Notes (Problems, Consultations, Changes, etc.):				Stable Name / Address:		

CLIENT INFORMATION	Name:	
	Address:	
	Phone:	Email:

HORSE INFORMATION	Name:	Breed:
	Gender:	Primary Use:
	Age:	Temperament (1-10):

Veterinarian:	HOOF ANGLES			HOOF LENGTHS		
		Left	Right		Left	Right
Trainer:	Front			Front		
	Back			Back		
Health Concerns:	Supplements:			Shoe Size:		
				Shoe Type:		
				Shoe Pads:		
Therapeutic Treatments:	Special Requirements:			Dates Due:		
Notes (Problems, Consultations, Changes, etc.):				Stable Name / Address:		

CLIENT INFORMATION	Name:		
	Address:		
	Phone:		Email:

HORSE INFORMATION	Name:		Breed:
	Gender:		Primary Use:
	Age:		Temperament (1-10):

Veterinarian:	HOOF ANGLES			HOOF LENGTHS		
		Left	Right		Left	Right
Trainer:	Front			Front		
	Back			Back		

Health Concerns:	Supplements:	Shoe Size:
		Shoe Type:
		Shoe Pads:
Therapeutic Treatments:	Special Requirements:	Dates Due:

Notes (Problems, Consultations, Changes, etc.):	Stable Name / Address:

CLIENT INFORMATION	Name:		
	Address:		
	Phone:		Email:

HORSE INFORMATION	Name:		Breed:
	Gender:		Primary Use:
	Age:		Temperament (1-10):

Veterinarian:	HOOF ANGLES			HOOF LENGTHS		
		Left	Right		Left	Right
Trainer:	Front			Front		
	Back			Back		

Health Concerns:	Supplements:	Shoe Size:
		Shoe Type:
		Shoe Pads:
Therapeutic Treatments:	Special Requirements:	Dates Due:

Notes (Problems, Consultations, Changes, etc.):	Stable Name / Address:

CLIENT INFORMATION	Name:						
	Address:						
	Phone:			Email:			
HORSE INFORMATION	Name:			Breed:			
	Gender:			Primary Use:			
	Age:			Temperament (1-10):			
Veterinarian:	HOOF ANGLES			HOOF LENGTHS			
		Left	Right			Left	Right
Trainer:	Front				Front		
	Back				Back		
Health Concerns:	Supplements:			Shoe Size:			
				Shoe Type:			
				Shoe Pads:			
Therapeutic Treatments:	Special Requirements:			Dates Due:			
Notes (Problems, Consultations, Changes, etc.):				Stable Name / Address:			

CLIENT INFORMATION	Name:						
	Address:						
	Phone:			Email:			
HORSE INFORMATION	Name:			Breed:			
	Gender:			Primary Use:			
	Age:			Temperament (1-10):			
Veterinarian:	HOOF ANGLES			HOOF LENGTHS			
		Left	Right			Left	Right
Trainer:	Front				Front		
	Back				Back		
Health Concerns:	Supplements:			Shoe Size:			
				Shoe Type:			
				Shoe Pads:			
Therapeutic Treatments:	Special Requirements:			Dates Due:			
Notes (Problems, Consultations, Changes, etc.):				Stable Name / Address:			

Form 1

CLIENT INFORMATION	Name:		
	Address:		
	Phone:	Email:	

HORSE INFORMATION	Name:	Breed:	
	Gender:	Primary Use:	
	Age:	Temperament (1-10):	

Veterinarian:

HOOF ANGLES			HOOF LENGTHS		
	Left	Right		Left	Right
Front			Front		
Back			Back		

Trainer:

Health Concerns:

Supplements:

Shoe Size:
Shoe Type:
Shoe Pads:

Therapeutic Treatments:

Special Requirements:

Dates Due:

Notes (Problems, Consultations, Changes, etc.):

Stable Name / Address:

Form 2

CLIENT INFORMATION	Name:		
	Address:		
	Phone:	Email:	

HORSE INFORMATION	Name:	Breed:	
	Gender:	Primary Use:	
	Age:	Temperament (1-10):	

Veterinarian:

HOOF ANGLES			HOOF LENGTHS		
	Left	Right		Left	Right
Front			Front		
Back			Back		

Trainer:

Health Concerns:

Supplements:

Shoe Size:
Shoe Type:
Shoe Pads:

Therapeutic Treatments:

Special Requirements:

Dates Due:

Notes (Problems, Consultations, Changes, etc.):

Stable Name / Address:

CLIENT INFORMATION	Name:						
	Address:						
	Phone:				Email:		
HORSE INFORMATION	Name:				Breed:		
	Gender:				Primary Use:		
	Age:				Temperament (1-10):		

Veterinarian:	HOOF ANGLES			HOOF LENGTHS		
		Left	Right		Left	Right
Trainer:	Front			Front		
	Back			Back		
Health Concerns:	Supplements:			Shoe Size:		
				Shoe Type:		
				Shoe Pads:		
Therapeutic Treatments:	Special Requirements:			Dates Due:		
Notes (Problems, Consultations, Changes, etc.):				Stable Name / Address:		

CLIENT INFORMATION	Name:						
	Address:						
	Phone:				Email:		
HORSE INFORMATION	Name:				Breed:		
	Gender:				Primary Use:		
	Age:				Temperament (1-10):		

Veterinarian:	HOOF ANGLES			HOOF LENGTHS		
		Left	Right		Left	Right
Trainer:	Front			Front		
	Back			Back		
Health Concerns:	Supplements:			Shoe Size:		
				Shoe Type:		
				Shoe Pads:		
Therapeutic Treatments:	Special Requirements:			Dates Due:		
Notes (Problems, Consultations, Changes, etc.):				Stable Name / Address:		

CLIENT INFORMATION	Name:			
	Address:			
	Phone:		Email:	

HORSE INFORMATION	Name:		Breed:	
	Gender:		Primary Use:	
	Age:		Temperament (1-10):	

Veterinarian:	HOOF ANGLES			HOOF LENGTHS		
		Left	Right		Left	Right
Trainer:	Front			Front		
	Back			Back		

Health Concerns:	Supplements:	Shoe Size:
		Shoe Type:
		Shoe Pads:
Therapeutic Treatments:	Special Requirements:	Dates Due:
Notes (Problems, Consultations, Changes, etc.):		Stable Name / Address:

CLIENT INFORMATION	Name:			
	Address:			
	Phone:		Email:	

HORSE INFORMATION	Name:		Breed:	
	Gender:		Primary Use:	
	Age:		Temperament (1-10):	

Veterinarian:	HOOF ANGLES			HOOF LENGTHS		
		Left	Right		Left	Right
Trainer:	Front			Front		
	Back			Back		

Health Concerns:	Supplements:	Shoe Size:
		Shoe Type:
		Shoe Pads:
Therapeutic Treatments:	Special Requirements:	Dates Due:
Notes (Problems, Consultations, Changes, etc.):		Stable Name / Address:

CLIENT INFORMATION	Name:						
	Address:						
	Phone:			Email:			
HORSE INFORMATION	Name:			Breed:			
	Gender:			Primary Use:			
	Age:			Temperament (1-10):			

Veterinarian:	HOOF ANGLES			HOOF LENGTHS		
		Left	Right		Left	Right
Trainer:	Front			Front		
	Back			Back		

Health Concerns:	Supplements:	Shoe Size:
		Shoe Type:
		Shoe Pads:
Therapeutic Treatments:	Special Requirements:	Dates Due:
Notes (Problems, Consultations, Changes, etc.):		Stable Name / Address:

CLIENT INFORMATION	Name:						
	Address:						
	Phone:			Email:			
HORSE INFORMATION	Name:			Breed:			
	Gender:			Primary Use:			
	Age:			Temperament (1-10):			

Veterinarian:	HOOF ANGLES			HOOF LENGTHS		
		Left	Right		Left	Right
Trainer:	Front			Front		
	Back			Back		

Health Concerns:	Supplements:	Shoe Size:
		Shoe Type:
		Shoe Pads:
Therapeutic Treatments:	Special Requirements:	Dates Due:
Notes (Problems, Consultations, Changes, etc.):		Stable Name / Address:

CLIENT INFORMATION	Name:			
	Address:			
	Phone:		Email:	

HORSE INFORMATION	Name:		Breed:	
	Gender:		Primary Use:	
	Age:		Temperament (1-10):	

Veterinarian:

HOOF ANGLES			HOOF LENGTHS		
	Left	Right		Left	Right
Front			Front		
Back			Back		

Trainer:

Health Concerns:	Supplements:	Shoe Size:
		Shoe Type:
		Shoe Pads:
Therapeutic Treatments:	Special Requirements:	Dates Due:
Notes (Problems, Consultations, Changes, etc.):		Stable Name / Address:

CLIENT INFORMATION	Name:			
	Address:			
	Phone:		Email:	

HORSE INFORMATION	Name:		Breed:	
	Gender:		Primary Use:	
	Age:		Temperament (1-10):	

Veterinarian:

HOOF ANGLES			HOOF LENGTHS		
	Left	Right		Left	Right
Front			Front		
Back			Back		

Trainer:

Health Concerns:	Supplements:	Shoe Size:
		Shoe Type:
		Shoe Pads:
Therapeutic Treatments:	Special Requirements:	Dates Due:
Notes (Problems, Consultations, Changes, etc.):		Stable Name / Address:

CLIENT INFORMATION	Name:						
	Address:						
	Phone:			Email:			
HORSE INFORMATION	Name:			Breed:			
	Gender:			Primary Use:			
	Age:			Temperament (1-10):			

Veterinarian:	HOOF ANGLES			HOOF LENGTHS		
		Left	Right		Left	Right
Trainer:	Front			Front		
	Back			Back		
Health Concerns:	Supplements:			Shoe Size:		
				Shoe Type:		
				Shoe Pads:		
Therapeutic Treatments:	Special Requirements:			Dates Due:		
Notes (Problems, Consultations, Changes, etc.):				Stable Name / Address:		

CLIENT INFORMATION	Name:						
	Address:						
	Phone:			Email:			
HORSE INFORMATION	Name:			Breed:			
	Gender:			Primary Use:			
	Age:			Temperament (1-10):			

Veterinarian:	HOOF ANGLES			HOOF LENGTHS		
		Left	Right		Left	Right
Trainer:	Front			Front		
	Back			Back		
Health Concerns:	Supplements:			Shoe Size:		
				Shoe Type:		
				Shoe Pads:		
Therapeutic Treatments:	Special Requirements:			Dates Due:		
Notes (Problems, Consultations, Changes, etc.):				Stable Name / Address:		

CLIENT INFORMATION	Name:						
	Address:						
	Phone:			Email:			
HORSE INFORMATION	Name:			Breed:			
	Gender:			Primary Use:			
	Age:			Temperament (1-10):			

Veterinarian:	HOOF ANGLES			HOOF LENGTHS		
		Left	Right		Left	Right
Trainer:	Front			Front		
	Back			Back		
Health Concerns:	Supplements:			Shoe Size:		
				Shoe Type:		
				Shoe Pads:		
Therapeutic Treatments:	Special Requirements:			Dates Due:		
Notes (Problems, Consultations, Changes, etc.):				Stable Name / Address:		

CLIENT INFORMATION	Name:						
	Address:						
	Phone:			Email:			
HORSE INFORMATION	Name:			Breed:			
	Gender:			Primary Use:			
	Age:			Temperament (1-10):			

Veterinarian:	HOOF ANGLES			HOOF LENGTHS		
		Left	Right		Left	Right
Trainer:	Front			Front		
	Back			Back		
Health Concerns:	Supplements:			Shoe Size:		
				Shoe Type:		
				Shoe Pads:		
Therapeutic Treatments:	Special Requirements:			Dates Due:		
Notes (Problems, Consultations, Changes, etc.):				Stable Name / Address:		

CLIENT INFORMATION	Name:					
	Address:					
	Phone:			Email:		
HORSE INFORMATION	Name:			Breed:		
	Gender:			Primary Use:		
	Age:			Temperament (1-10):		

Veterinarian:	HOOF ANGLES			HOOF LENGTHS		
		Left	Right		Left	Right
Trainer:	Front			Front		
	Back			Back		
Health Concerns:	Supplements:			Shoe Size:		
				Shoe Type:		
				Shoe Pads:		
Therapeutic Treatments:	Special Requirements:			Dates Due:		
Notes (Problems, Consultations, Changes, etc.):				Stable Name / Address:		

CLIENT INFORMATION	Name:					
	Address:					
	Phone:			Email:		
HORSE INFORMATION	Name:			Breed:		
	Gender:			Primary Use:		
	Age:			Temperament (1-10):		

Veterinarian:	HOOF ANGLES			HOOF LENGTHS		
		Left	Right		Left	Right
Trainer:	Front			Front		
	Back			Back		
Health Concerns:	Supplements:			Shoe Size:		
				Shoe Type:		
				Shoe Pads:		
Therapeutic Treatments:	Special Requirements:			Dates Due:		
Notes (Problems, Consultations, Changes, etc.):				Stable Name / Address:		

CLIENT INFORMATION	Name:						
	Address:						
	Phone:				Email:		
HORSE INFORMATION	Name:				Breed:		
	Gender:				Primary Use:		
	Age:				Temperament (1-10):		

Veterinarian:	HOOF ANGLES			HOOF LENGTHS		
		Left	Right		Left	Right
Trainer:	Front			Front		
	Back			Back		
Health Concerns:	Supplements:			Shoe Size:		
				Shoe Type:		
				Shoe Pads:		
Therapeutic Treatments:	Special Requirements:			Dates Due:		
Notes (Problems, Consultations, Changes, etc.):				Stable Name / Address:		

CLIENT INFORMATION	Name:						
	Address:						
	Phone:				Email:		
HORSE INFORMATION	Name:				Breed:		
	Gender:				Primary Use:		
	Age:				Temperament (1-10):		

Veterinarian:	HOOF ANGLES			HOOF LENGTHS		
		Left	Right		Left	Right
Trainer:	Front			Front		
	Back			Back		
Health Concerns:	Supplements:			Shoe Size:		
				Shoe Type:		
				Shoe Pads:		
Therapeutic Treatments:	Special Requirements:			Dates Due:		
Notes (Problems, Consultations, Changes, etc.):				Stable Name / Address:		

CLIENT INFORMATION	Name:		
	Address:		
	Phone:		Email:

HORSE INFORMATION	Name:		Breed:
	Gender:		Primary Use:
	Age:		Temperament (1-10):

Veterinarian:	HOOF ANGLES			HOOF LENGTHS		
		Left	Right		Left	Right
Trainer:	Front			Front		
	Back			Back		

Health Concerns:	Supplements:	Shoe Size:
		Shoe Type:
		Shoe Pads:
Therapeutic Treatments:	Special Requirements:	Dates Due:

| Notes (Problems, Consultations, Changes, etc.): | Stable Name / Address: |

CLIENT INFORMATION	Name:		
	Address:		
	Phone:		Email:

HORSE INFORMATION	Name:		Breed:
	Gender:		Primary Use:
	Age:		Temperament (1-10):

Veterinarian:	HOOF ANGLES			HOOF LENGTHS		
		Left	Right		Left	Right
Trainer:	Front			Front		
	Back			Back		

Health Concerns:	Supplements:	Shoe Size:
		Shoe Type:
		Shoe Pads:
Therapeutic Treatments:	Special Requirements:	Dates Due:

| Notes (Problems, Consultations, Changes, etc.): | Stable Name / Address: |

CLIENT INFORMATION	Name:						
	Address:						
	Phone:			Email:			

HORSE INFORMATION	Name:			Breed:			
	Gender:			Primary Use:			
	Age:			Temperament (1-10):			

Veterinarian:	HOOF ANGLES			HOOF LENGTHS			
		Left	Right			Left	Right
Trainer:	Front				Front		
	Back				Back		
Health Concerns:	Supplements:			Shoe Size:			
				Shoe Type:			
				Shoe Pads:			
Therapeutic Treatments:	Special Requirements:			Dates Due:			
Notes (Problems, Consultations, Changes, etc.):				Stable Name / Address:			

CLIENT INFORMATION	Name:						
	Address:						
	Phone:			Email:			

HORSE INFORMATION	Name:			Breed:			
	Gender:			Primary Use:			
	Age:			Temperament (1-10):			

Veterinarian:	HOOF ANGLES			HOOF LENGTHS			
		Left	Right			Left	Right
Trainer:	Front				Front		
	Back				Back		
Health Concerns:	Supplements:			Shoe Size:			
				Shoe Type:			
				Shoe Pads:			
Therapeutic Treatments:	Special Requirements:			Dates Due:			
Notes (Problems, Consultations, Changes, etc.):				Stable Name / Address:			

CLIENT INFORMATION	Name:	
	Address:	
	Phone:	Email:

HORSE INFORMATION	Name:	Breed:
	Gender:	Primary Use:
	Age:	Temperament (1-10):

Veterinarian:	HOOF ANGLES			HOOF LENGTHS		
		Left	Right		Left	Right
Trainer:	Front			Front		
	Back			Back		
Health Concerns:	Supplements:			Shoe Size:		
				Shoe Type:		
				Shoe Pads:		
Therapeutic Treatments:	Special Requirements:			Dates Due:		
Notes (Problems, Consultations, Changes, etc.):				Stable Name / Address:		

CLIENT INFORMATION	Name:	
	Address:	
	Phone:	Email:

HORSE INFORMATION	Name:	Breed:
	Gender:	Primary Use:
	Age:	Temperament (1-10):

Veterinarian:	HOOF ANGLES			HOOF LENGTHS		
		Left	Right		Left	Right
Trainer:	Front			Front		
	Back			Back		
Health Concerns:	Supplements:			Shoe Size:		
				Shoe Type:		
				Shoe Pads:		
Therapeutic Treatments:	Special Requirements:			Dates Due:		
Notes (Problems, Consultations, Changes, etc.):				Stable Name / Address:		

CLIENT INFORMATION	Name:	
	Address:	
	Phone:	Email:

HORSE INFORMATION	Name:	Breed:
	Gender:	Primary Use:
	Age:	Temperament (1-10):

Veterinarian:	HOOF ANGLES			HOOF LENGTHS		
		Left	Right		Left	Right
Trainer:	Front			Front		
	Back			Back		

Health Concerns:	Supplements:	Shoe Size:
		Shoe Type:
		Shoe Pads:
Therapeutic Treatments:	Special Requirements:	Dates Due:

| Notes (Problems, Consultations, Changes, etc.): | Stable Name / Address: |

CLIENT INFORMATION	Name:	
	Address:	
	Phone:	Email:

HORSE INFORMATION	Name:	Breed:
	Gender:	Primary Use:
	Age:	Temperament (1-10):

Veterinarian:	HOOF ANGLES			HOOF LENGTHS		
		Left	Right		Left	Right
Trainer:	Front			Front		
	Back			Back		

Health Concerns:	Supplements:	Shoe Size:
		Shoe Type:
		Shoe Pads:
Therapeutic Treatments:	Special Requirements:	Dates Due:

| Notes (Problems, Consultations, Changes, etc.): | Stable Name / Address: |

CLIENT INFORMATION	Name:						
	Address:						
	Phone:			Email:			
HORSE INFORMATION	Name:			Breed:			
	Gender:			Primary Use:			
	Age:			Temperament (1-10):			

Veterinarian:	HOOF ANGLES			HOOF LENGTHS		
		Left	Right		Left	Right
Trainer:	Front			Front		
	Back			Back		
Health Concerns:	Supplements:			Shoe Size:		
				Shoe Type:		
				Shoe Pads:		
Therapeutic Treatments:	Special Requirements:			Dates Due:		
Notes (Problems, Consultations, Changes, etc.):				Stable Name / Address:		

CLIENT INFORMATION	Name:						
	Address:						
	Phone:			Email:			
HORSE INFORMATION	Name:			Breed:			
	Gender:			Primary Use:			
	Age:			Temperament (1-10):			

Veterinarian:	HOOF ANGLES			HOOF LENGTHS		
		Left	Right		Left	Right
Trainer:	Front			Front		
	Back			Back		
Health Concerns:	Supplements:			Shoe Size:		
				Shoe Type:		
				Shoe Pads:		
Therapeutic Treatments:	Special Requirements:			Dates Due:		
Notes (Problems, Consultations, Changes, etc.):				Stable Name / Address:		

CLIENT INFORMATION	Name:		
	Address:		
	Phone:		Email:

HORSE INFORMATION	Name:		Breed:
	Gender:		Primary Use:
	Age:		Temperament (1-10):

Veterinarian:	HOOF ANGLES			HOOF LENGTHS		
		Left	Right		Left	Right
Trainer:	Front			Front		
	Back			Back		
Health Concerns:	Supplements:			Shoe Size:		
				Shoe Type:		
				Shoe Pads:		
Therapeutic Treatments:	Special Requirements:			Dates Due:		
Notes (Problems, Consultations, Changes, etc.):				Stable Name / Address:		

CLIENT INFORMATION	Name:		
	Address:		
	Phone:		Email:

HORSE INFORMATION	Name:		Breed:
	Gender:		Primary Use:
	Age:		Temperament (1-10):

Veterinarian:	HOOF ANGLES			HOOF LENGTHS		
		Left	Right		Left	Right
Trainer:	Front			Front		
	Back			Back		
Health Concerns:	Supplements:			Shoe Size:		
				Shoe Type:		
				Shoe Pads:		
Therapeutic Treatments:	Special Requirements:			Dates Due:		
Notes (Problems, Consultations, Changes, etc.):				Stable Name / Address:		

CLIENT INFORMATION	Name:	
	Address:	
	Phone:	Email:

HORSE INFORMATION	Name:	Breed:
	Gender:	Primary Use:
	Age:	Temperament (1-10):

Veterinarian:	HOOF ANGLES			HOOF LENGTHS		
		Left	Right		Left	Right
Trainer:	Front			Front		
	Back			Back		

Health Concerns:	Supplements:	Shoe Size:
		Shoe Type:
		Shoe Pads:
Therapeutic Treatments:	Special Requirements:	Dates Due:

Notes (Problems, Consultations, Changes, etc.):	Stable Name / Address:

CLIENT INFORMATION	Name:	
	Address:	
	Phone:	Email:

HORSE INFORMATION	Name:	Breed:
	Gender:	Primary Use:
	Age:	Temperament (1-10):

Veterinarian:	HOOF ANGLES			HOOF LENGTHS		
		Left	Right		Left	Right
Trainer:	Front			Front		
	Back			Back		

Health Concerns:	Supplements:	Shoe Size:
		Shoe Type:
		Shoe Pads:
Therapeutic Treatments:	Special Requirements:	Dates Due:

Notes (Problems, Consultations, Changes, etc.):	Stable Name / Address:

CLIENT INFORMATION	Name:						
	Address:						
	Phone:			Email:			
HORSE INFORMATION	Name:			Breed:			
	Gender:			Primary Use:			
	Age:			Temperament (1-10):			

Veterinarian:	HOOF ANGLES			HOOF LENGTHS		
		Left	Right		Left	Right
Trainer:	Front			Front		
	Back			Back		
Health Concerns:	Supplements:			Shoe Size:		
				Shoe Type:		
				Shoe Pads:		
Therapeutic Treatments:	Special Requirements:			Dates Due:		
Notes (Problems, Consultations, Changes, etc.):				Stable Name / Address:		

CLIENT INFORMATION	Name:						
	Address:						
	Phone:			Email:			
HORSE INFORMATION	Name:			Breed:			
	Gender:			Primary Use:			
	Age:			Temperament (1-10):			

Veterinarian:	HOOF ANGLES			HOOF LENGTHS		
		Left	Right		Left	Right
Trainer:	Front			Front		
	Back			Back		
Health Concerns:	Supplements:			Shoe Size:		
				Shoe Type:		
				Shoe Pads:		
Therapeutic Treatments:	Special Requirements:			Dates Due:		
Notes (Problems, Consultations, Changes, etc.):				Stable Name / Address:		

CLIENT INFORMATION	Name:	
	Address:	
	Phone:	Email:

HORSE INFORMATION	Name:	Breed:
	Gender:	Primary Use:
	Age:	Temperament (1-10):

Veterinarian:	HOOF ANGLES			HOOF LENGTHS		
		Left	Right		Left	Right
Trainer:	Front			Front		
	Back			Back		

Health Concerns:	Supplements:	Shoe Size:
		Shoe Type:
		Shoe Pads:
Therapeutic Treatments:	Special Requirements:	Dates Due:
Notes (Problems, Consultations, Changes, etc.):		Stable Name / Address:

CLIENT INFORMATION	Name:	
	Address:	
	Phone:	Email:

HORSE INFORMATION	Name:	Breed:
	Gender:	Primary Use:
	Age:	Temperament (1-10):

Veterinarian:	HOOF ANGLES			HOOF LENGTHS		
		Left	Right		Left	Right
Trainer:	Front			Front		
	Back			Back		

Health Concerns:	Supplements:	Shoe Size:
		Shoe Type:
		Shoe Pads:
Therapeutic Treatments:	Special Requirements:	Dates Due:
Notes (Problems, Consultations, Changes, etc.):		Stable Name / Address:

CLIENT INFORMATION	Name:						
	Address:						
	Phone:			Email:			
HORSE INFORMATION	Name:			Breed:			
	Gender:			Primary Use:			
	Age:			Temperament (1-10):			

Veterinarian:	HOOF ANGLES			HOOF LENGTHS		
		Left	Right		Left	Right
Trainer:	Front			Front		
	Back			Back		

Health Concerns:	Supplements:	Shoe Size:
		Shoe Type:
		Shoe Pads:
Therapeutic Treatments:	Special Requirements:	Dates Due:
Notes (Problems, Consultations, Changes, etc.):		Stable Name / Address:

CLIENT INFORMATION	Name:						
	Address:						
	Phone:			Email:			
HORSE INFORMATION	Name:			Breed:			
	Gender:			Primary Use:			
	Age:			Temperament (1-10):			

Veterinarian:	HOOF ANGLES			HOOF LENGTHS		
		Left	Right		Left	Right
Trainer:	Front			Front		
	Back			Back		

Health Concerns:	Supplements:	Shoe Size:
		Shoe Type:
		Shoe Pads:
Therapeutic Treatments:	Special Requirements:	Dates Due:
Notes (Problems, Consultations, Changes, etc.):		Stable Name / Address:

CLIENT INFORMATION	Name:						
	Address:						
	Phone:			Email:			
HORSE INFORMATION	Name:			Breed:			
	Gender:			Primary Use:			
	Age:			Temperament (1-10):			
Veterinarian:	HOOF ANGLES			HOOF LENGTHS			
		Left	Right		Left	Right	
Trainer:	Front			Front			
	Back			Back			
Health Concerns:	Supplements:			Shoe Size:			
				Shoe Type:			
				Shoe Pads:			
Therapeutic Treatments:	Special Requirements:			Dates Due:			
Notes (Problems, Consultations, Changes, etc.):				Stable Name / Address:			

CLIENT INFORMATION	Name:						
	Address:						
	Phone:			Email:			
HORSE INFORMATION	Name:			Breed:			
	Gender:			Primary Use:			
	Age:			Temperament (1-10):			
Veterinarian:	HOOF ANGLES			HOOF LENGTHS			
		Left	Right		Left	Right	
Trainer:	Front			Front			
	Back			Back			
Health Concerns:	Supplements:			Shoe Size:			
				Shoe Type:			
				Shoe Pads:			
Therapeutic Treatments:	Special Requirements:			Dates Due:			
Notes (Problems, Consultations, Changes, etc.):				Stable Name / Address:			

CLIENT INFORMATION	Name:						
	Address:						
	Phone:			Email:			
HORSE INFORMATION	Name:			Breed:			
	Gender:			Primary Use:			
	Age:			Temperament (1-10):			

Veterinarian:	HOOF ANGLES			HOOF LENGTHS			
		Left	Right			Left	Right
Trainer:	Front				Front		
	Back				Back		
Health Concerns:	Supplements:			Shoe Size:			
				Shoe Type:			
				Shoe Pads:			
Therapeutic Treatments:	Special Requirements:			Dates Due:			
Notes (Problems, Consultations, Changes, etc.):				Stable Name / Address:			

CLIENT INFORMATION	Name:						
	Address:						
	Phone:			Email:			
HORSE INFORMATION	Name:			Breed:			
	Gender:			Primary Use:			
	Age:			Temperament (1-10):			

Veterinarian:	HOOF ANGLES			HOOF LENGTHS			
		Left	Right			Left	Right
Trainer:	Front				Front		
	Back				Back		
Health Concerns:	Supplements:			Shoe Size:			
				Shoe Type:			
				Shoe Pads:			
Therapeutic Treatments:	Special Requirements:			Dates Due:			
Notes (Problems, Consultations, Changes, etc.):				Stable Name / Address:			

CLIENT INFORMATION	Name:						
	Address:						
	Phone:			Email:			
HORSE INFORMATION	Name:			Breed:			
	Gender:			Primary Use:			
	Age:			Temperament (1-10):			

Veterinarian:	HOOF ANGLES			HOOF LENGTHS		
		Left	Right		Left	Right
Trainer:	Front			Front		
	Back			Back		
Health Concerns:	Supplements:			Shoe Size:		
				Shoe Type:		
				Shoe Pads:		
Therapeutic Treatments:	Special Requirements:			Dates Due:		
Notes (Problems, Consultations, Changes, etc.):				Stable Name / Address:		

CLIENT INFORMATION	Name:						
	Address:						
	Phone:			Email:			
HORSE INFORMATION	Name:			Breed:			
	Gender:			Primary Use:			
	Age:			Temperament (1-10):			

Veterinarian:	HOOF ANGLES			HOOF LENGTHS		
		Left	Right		Left	Right
Trainer:	Front			Front		
	Back			Back		
Health Concerns:	Supplements:			Shoe Size:		
				Shoe Type:		
				Shoe Pads:		
Therapeutic Treatments:	Special Requirements:			Dates Due:		
Notes (Problems, Consultations, Changes, etc.):				Stable Name / Address:		

CLIENT INFORMATION	Name:		
	Address:		
	Phone:		Email:
HORSE INFORMATION	Name:		Breed:
	Gender:		Primary Use:
	Age:		Temperament (1-10):

Veterinarian:	HOOF ANGLES			HOOF LENGTHS		
		Left	Right		Left	Right
Trainer:	Front			Front		
	Back			Back		

Health Concerns:	Supplements:	Shoe Size:
		Shoe Type:
		Shoe Pads:
Therapeutic Treatments:	Special Requirements:	Dates Due:
Notes (Problems, Consultations, Changes, etc.):		Stable Name / Address:

CLIENT INFORMATION	Name:		
	Address:		
	Phone:		Email:
HORSE INFORMATION	Name:		Breed:
	Gender:		Primary Use:
	Age:		Temperament (1-10):

Veterinarian:	HOOF ANGLES			HOOF LENGTHS		
		Left	Right		Left	Right
Trainer:	Front			Front		
	Back			Back		

Health Concerns:	Supplements:	Shoe Size:
		Shoe Type:
		Shoe Pads:
Therapeutic Treatments:	Special Requirements:	Dates Due:
Notes (Problems, Consultations, Changes, etc.):		Stable Name / Address:

CLIENT INFORMATION	Name:	
	Address:	
	Phone:	Email:

HORSE INFORMATION	Name:	Breed:
	Gender:	Primary Use:
	Age:	Temperament (1-10):

Veterinarian:	HOOF ANGLES			HOOF LENGTHS		
		Left	Right		Left	Right
Trainer:	Front			Front		
	Back			Back		

Health Concerns:	Supplements:	Shoe Size:
		Shoe Type:
		Shoe Pads:

Therapeutic Treatments:	Special Requirements:	Dates Due:

Notes (Problems, Consultations, Changes, etc.):	Stable Name / Address:

CLIENT INFORMATION	Name:	
	Address:	
	Phone:	Email:

HORSE INFORMATION	Name:	Breed:
	Gender:	Primary Use:
	Age:	Temperament (1-10):

Veterinarian:	HOOF ANGLES			HOOF LENGTHS		
		Left	Right		Left	Right
Trainer:	Front			Front		
	Back			Back		

Health Concerns:	Supplements:	Shoe Size:
		Shoe Type:
		Shoe Pads:

Therapeutic Treatments:	Special Requirements:	Dates Due:

Notes (Problems, Consultations, Changes, etc.):	Stable Name / Address:

CLIENT INFORMATION	Name:	
	Address:	
	Phone:	Email:

HORSE INFORMATION	Name:	Breed:
	Gender:	Primary Use:
	Age:	Temperament (1-10):

Veterinarian:

HOOF ANGLES			HOOF LENGTHS		
	Left	Right		Left	Right
Front			Front		
Back			Back		

Trainer:

Health Concerns:	Supplements:	Shoe Size:
		Shoe Type:
		Shoe Pads:

Therapeutic Treatments:	Special Requirements:	Dates Due:

Notes (Problems, Consultations, Changes, etc.):	Stable Name / Address:

CLIENT INFORMATION	Name:	
	Address:	
	Phone:	Email:

HORSE INFORMATION	Name:	Breed:
	Gender:	Primary Use:
	Age:	Temperament (1-10):

Veterinarian:

HOOF ANGLES			HOOF LENGTHS		
	Left	Right		Left	Right
Front			Front		
Back			Back		

Trainer:

Health Concerns:	Supplements:	Shoe Size:
		Shoe Type:
		Shoe Pads:

Therapeutic Treatments:	Special Requirements:	Dates Due:

Notes (Problems, Consultations, Changes, etc.):	Stable Name / Address:

CLIENT INFORMATION	Name:						
	Address:						
	Phone:			Email:			
HORSE INFORMATION	Name:			Breed:			
	Gender:			Primary Use:			
	Age:			Temperament (1-10):			

Veterinarian:	HOOF ANGLES			HOOF LENGTHS		
		Left	Right		Left	Right
Trainer:	Front			Front		
	Back			Back		
Health Concerns:	Supplements:			Shoe Size:		
				Shoe Type:		
				Shoe Pads:		
Therapeutic Treatments:	Special Requirements:			Dates Due:		
Notes (Problems, Consultations, Changes, etc.):				Stable Name / Address:		

CLIENT INFORMATION	Name:						
	Address:						
	Phone:			Email:			
HORSE INFORMATION	Name:			Breed:			
	Gender:			Primary Use:			
	Age:			Temperament (1-10):			

Veterinarian:	HOOF ANGLES			HOOF LENGTHS		
		Left	Right		Left	Right
Trainer:	Front			Front		
	Back			Back		
Health Concerns:	Supplements:			Shoe Size:		
				Shoe Type:		
				Shoe Pads:		
Therapeutic Treatments:	Special Requirements:			Dates Due:		
Notes (Problems, Consultations, Changes, etc.):				Stable Name / Address:		

CLIENT INFORMATION	Name:						
	Address:						
	Phone:				Email:		
HORSE INFORMATION	Name:				Breed:		
	Gender:				Primary Use:		
	Age:				Temperament (1-10):		

Veterinarian:	HOOF ANGLES			HOOF LENGTHS		
		Left	Right		Left	Right
Trainer:	Front			Front		
	Back			Back		
Health Concerns:	Supplements:			Shoe Size:		
				Shoe Type:		
				Shoe Pads:		
Therapeutic Treatments:	Special Requirements:			Dates Due:		
Notes (Problems, Consultations, Changes, etc.):				Stable Name / Address:		

CLIENT INFORMATION	Name:						
	Address:						
	Phone:				Email:		
HORSE INFORMATION	Name:				Breed:		
	Gender:				Primary Use:		
	Age:				Temperament (1-10):		

Veterinarian:	HOOF ANGLES			HOOF LENGTHS		
		Left	Right		Left	Right
Trainer:	Front			Front		
	Back			Back		
Health Concerns:	Supplements:			Shoe Size:		
				Shoe Type:		
				Shoe Pads:		
Therapeutic Treatments:	Special Requirements:			Dates Due:		
Notes (Problems, Consultations, Changes, etc.):				Stable Name / Address:		

CLIENT INFORMATION	Name:						
	Address:						
	Phone:				Email:		
HORSE INFORMATION	Name:				Breed:		
	Gender:				Primary Use:		
	Age:				Temperament (1-10):		

Veterinarian:	HOOF ANGLES			HOOF LENGTHS		
		Left	Right		Left	Right
Trainer:	Front			Front		
	Back			Back		
Health Concerns:	Supplements:			Shoe Size:		
				Shoe Type:		
				Shoe Pads:		
Therapeutic Treatments:	Special Requirements:			Dates Due:		
Notes (Problems, Consultations, Changes, etc.):				Stable Name / Address:		

CLIENT INFORMATION	Name:						
	Address:						
	Phone:				Email:		
HORSE INFORMATION	Name:				Breed:		
	Gender:				Primary Use:		
	Age:				Temperament (1-10):		

Veterinarian:	HOOF ANGLES			HOOF LENGTHS		
		Left	Right		Left	Right
Trainer:	Front			Front		
	Back			Back		
Health Concerns:	Supplements:			Shoe Size:		
				Shoe Type:		
				Shoe Pads:		
Therapeutic Treatments:	Special Requirements:			Dates Due:		
Notes (Problems, Consultations, Changes, etc.):				Stable Name / Address:		

CLIENT INFORMATION	Name:						
	Address:						
	Phone:				Email:		

HORSE INFORMATION	Name:				Breed:		
	Gender:				Primary Use:		
	Age:				Temperament (1-10):		

Veterinarian:	HOOF ANGLES			HOOF LENGTHS			
		Left	Right			Left	Right
Trainer:	Front			Front			
	Back			Back			
Health Concerns:	Supplements:			Shoe Size:			
				Shoe Type:			
				Shoe Pads:			
Therapeutic Treatments:	Special Requirements:			Dates Due:			
Notes (Problems, Consultations, Changes, etc.):				Stable Name / Address:			

CLIENT INFORMATION	Name:						
	Address:						
	Phone:				Email:		

HORSE INFORMATION	Name:				Breed:		
	Gender:				Primary Use:		
	Age:				Temperament (1-10):		

Veterinarian:	HOOF ANGLES			HOOF LENGTHS			
		Left	Right			Left	Right
Trainer:	Front			Front			
	Back			Back			
Health Concerns:	Supplements:			Shoe Size:			
				Shoe Type:			
				Shoe Pads:			
Therapeutic Treatments:	Special Requirements:			Dates Due:			
Notes (Problems, Consultations, Changes, etc.):				Stable Name / Address:			

CLIENT INFORMATION	Name:						
	Address:						
	Phone:			Email:			
HORSE INFORMATION	Name:			Breed:			
	Gender:			Primary Use:			
	Age:			Temperament (1-10):			

Veterinarian:	HOOF ANGLES			HOOF LENGTHS		
		Left	Right		Left	Right
Trainer:	Front			Front		
	Back			Back		
Health Concerns:	Supplements:			Shoe Size:		
				Shoe Type:		
				Shoe Pads:		
Therapeutic Treatments:	Special Requirements:			Dates Due:		
Notes (Problems, Consultations, Changes, etc.):				Stable Name / Address:		

CLIENT INFORMATION	Name:						
	Address:						
	Phone:			Email:			
HORSE INFORMATION	Name:			Breed:			
	Gender:			Primary Use:			
	Age:			Temperament (1-10):			

Veterinarian:	HOOF ANGLES			HOOF LENGTHS		
		Left	Right		Left	Right
Trainer:	Front			Front		
	Back			Back		
Health Concerns:	Supplements:			Shoe Size:		
				Shoe Type:		
				Shoe Pads:		
Therapeutic Treatments:	Special Requirements:			Dates Due:		
Notes (Problems, Consultations, Changes, etc.):				Stable Name / Address:		

WEEKLY APPOINTMENT CALENDAR

When in doubt, let your
horse do the thinking.

	SUNDAY	MONDAY	TUESDAY	WEDNESDAY	THURSDAY	FRIDAY	SATURDAY
DATE:							
7:00 AM							
8:00 AM							
9:00 AM							
10:00 AM							
11:00 AM							
12:00 AM							
1:00 PM							
2:00 PM							
3:00 PM							
4:00 PM							
5:00 PM							
6:00 PM							
7:00 PM							

A life without horses is like taking a breath without air.

	SUNDAY	MONDAY	TUESDAY	WEDNESDAY	THURSDAY	FRIDAY	SATURDAY
DATE:							
7:00 AM							
8:00 AM							
9:00 AM							
10:00 AM							
11:00 AM							
12:00 AM							
1:00 PM							
2:00 PM							
3:00 PM							
4:00 PM							
5:00 PM							
6:00 PM							
7:00 PM							

	SUNDAY	MONDAY	TUESDAY	WEDNESDAY	THURSDAY	FRIDAY	SATURDAY
DATE:							
7:00 AM							
8:00 AM							
9:00 AM							
10:00 AM							
11:00 AM							
12:00 AM							
1:00 PM							
2:00 PM							
3:00 PM							
4:00 PM							
5:00 PM							
6:00 PM							
7:00 PM							

A horse never runs so fast as when he has other horses to catch up and outpace. - Ovid

	SUNDAY	MONDAY	TUESDAY	WEDNESDAY	THURSDAY	FRIDAY	SATURDAY
DATE:							
7:00 AM							
8:00 AM							
9:00 AM							
10:00 AM							
11:00 AM							
12:00 AM							
1:00 PM							
2:00 PM							
3:00 PM							
4:00 PM							
5:00 PM							
6:00 PM							
7:00 PM							

	SUNDAY	MONDAY	TUESDAY	WEDNESDAY	THURSDAY	FRIDAY	SATURDAY
DATE:							
7:00 AM							
8:00 AM							
9:00 AM							
10:00 AM							
11:00 AM							
12:00 AM							
1:00 PM							
2:00 PM							
3:00 PM							
4:00 PM							
5:00 PM							
6:00 PM							
7:00 PM							

To understand the soul of a horse is the closest human beings can come to knowing perfection.

	SUNDAY	MONDAY	TUESDAY	WEDNESDAY	THURSDAY	FRIDAY	SATURDAY
DATE:							
7:00 AM							
8:00 AM							
9:00 AM							
10:00 AM							
11:00 AM							
12:00 AM							
1:00 PM							
2:00 PM							
3:00 PM							
4:00 PM							
5:00 PM							
6:00 PM							
7:00 PM							

	SUNDAY	MONDAY	TUESDAY	WEDNESDAY	THURSDAY	FRIDAY	SATURDAY
DATE:							
7:00 AM							
8:00 AM							
9:00 AM							
10:00 AM							
11:00 AM							
12:00 AM							
1:00 PM							
2:00 PM							
3:00 PM							
4:00 PM							
5:00 PM							
6:00 PM							
7:00 PM							

Horses lend us the wings we lack. ~ Pam Brown

	SUNDAY	MONDAY	TUESDAY	WEDNESDAY	THURSDAY	FRIDAY	SATURDAY
DATE:							
7:00 AM							
8:00 AM							
9:00 AM							
10:00 AM							
11:00 AM							
12:00 AM							
1:00 PM							
2:00 PM							
3:00 PM							
4:00 PM							
5:00 PM							
6:00 PM							
7:00 PM							

	SUNDAY	MONDAY	TUESDAY	WEDNESDAY	THURSDAY	FRIDAY	SATURDAY
DATE:							
7:00 AM							
8:00 AM							
9:00 AM							
10:00 AM							
11:00 AM							
12:00 AM							
1:00 PM							
2:00 PM							
3:00 PM							
4:00 PM							
5:00 PM							
6:00 PM							
7:00 PM							

There is no place like home but the barn!

	SUNDAY	MONDAY	TUESDAY	WEDNESDAY	THURSDAY	FRIDAY	SATURDAY
DATE:							
7:00 AM							
8:00 AM							
9:00 AM							
10:00 AM							
11:00 AM							
12:00 AM							
1:00 PM							
2:00 PM							
3:00 PM							
4:00 PM							
5:00 PM							
6:00 PM							
7:00 PM							

	SUNDAY	MONDAY	TUESDAY	WEDNESDAY	THURSDAY	FRIDAY	SATURDAY
DATE:							
7:00 AM							
8:00 AM							
9:00 AM							
10:00 AM							
11:00 AM							
12:00 AM							
1:00 PM							
2:00 PM							
3:00 PM							
4:00 PM							
5:00 PM							
6:00 PM							
7:00 PM							

If you live a life without horses, you don't live a life at all.

	SUNDAY	MONDAY	TUESDAY	WEDNESDAY	THURSDAY	FRIDAY	SATURDAY
DATE:							
7:00 AM							
8:00 AM							
9:00 AM							
10:00 AM							
11:00 AM							
12:00 AM							
1:00 PM							
2:00 PM							
3:00 PM							
4:00 PM							
5:00 PM							
6:00 PM							
7:00 PM							

	SUNDAY	MONDAY	TUESDAY	WEDNESDAY	THURSDAY	FRIDAY	SATURDAY
DATE:							
7:00 AM							
8:00 AM							
9:00 AM							
10:00 AM							
11:00 AM							
12:00 AM							
1:00 PM							
2:00 PM							
3:00 PM							
4:00 PM							
5:00 PM							
6:00 PM							
7:00 PM							

I can make a general in five minutes but a good horse is hard to replace. ~ Abraham Lincoln

	SUNDAY	MONDAY	TUESDAY	WEDNESDAY	THURSDAY	FRIDAY	SATURDAY
DATE:							
7:00 AM							
8:00 AM							
9:00 AM							
10:00 AM							
11:00 AM							
12:00 AM							
1:00 PM							
2:00 PM							
3:00 PM							
4:00 PM							
5:00 PM							
6:00 PM							
7:00 PM							

DATE:	SUNDAY	MONDAY	TUESDAY	WEDNESDAY	THURSDAY	FRIDAY	SATURDAY
7:00 AM							
8:00 AM							
9:00 AM							
10:00 AM							
11:00 AM							
12:00 AM							
1:00 PM							
2:00 PM							
3:00 PM							
4:00 PM							
5:00 PM							
6:00 PM							
7:00 PM							

Horses make a landscape look beautiful. ~ Alice Walker

	SUNDAY	MONDAY	TUESDAY	WEDNESDAY	THURSDAY	FRIDAY	SATURDAY
DATE:							
7:00 AM							
8:00 AM							
9:00 AM							
10:00 AM							
11:00 AM							
12:00 AM							
1:00 PM							
2:00 PM							
3:00 PM							
4:00 PM							
5:00 PM							
6:00 PM							
7:00 PM							

	SUNDAY	MONDAY	TUESDAY	WEDNESDAY	THURSDAY	FRIDAY	SATURDAY
DATE:							
7:00 AM							
8:00 AM							
9:00 AM							
10:00 AM							
11:00 AM							
12:00 AM							
1:00 PM							
2:00 PM							
3:00 PM							
4:00 PM							
5:00 PM							
6:00 PM							
7:00 PM							

They say princes learn no art truly but the art of horsemanship. The reason is the brave beast is no flatterer. He will throw a prince as soon as his groom. ~ Ben Johnson

	SUNDAY	MONDAY	TUESDAY	WEDNESDAY	THURSDAY	FRIDAY	SATURDAY
DATE:							
7:00 AM							
8:00 AM							
9:00 AM							
10:00 AM							
11:00 AM							
12:00 AM							
1:00 PM							
2:00 PM							
3:00 PM							
4:00 PM							
5:00 PM							
6:00 PM							
7:00 PM							

	SUNDAY	MONDAY	TUESDAY	WEDNESDAY	THURSDAY	FRIDAY	SATURDAY
DATE:							
7:00 AM							
8:00 AM							
9:00 AM							
10:00 AM							
11:00 AM							
12:00 AM							
1:00 PM							
2:00 PM							
3:00 PM							
4:00 PM							
5:00 PM							
6:00 PM							
7:00 PM							

Dogs have owners. Horses have staff.

	SUNDAY	MONDAY	TUESDAY	WEDNESDAY	THURSDAY	FRIDAY	SATURDAY
DATE:							
7:00 AM							
8:00 AM							
9:00 AM							
10:00 AM							
11:00 AM							
12:00 AM							
1:00 PM							
2:00 PM							
3:00 PM							
4:00 PM							
5:00 PM							
6:00 PM							
7:00 PM							

	SUNDAY	MONDAY	TUESDAY	WEDNESDAY	THURSDAY	FRIDAY	SATURDAY
DATE:							
7:00 AM							
8:00 AM							
9:00 AM							
10:00 AM							
11:00 AM							
12:00 AM							
1:00 PM							
2:00 PM							
3:00 PM							
4:00 PM							
5:00 PM							
6:00 PM							
7:00 PM							

The horse can't talk but he can understand you!

	SUNDAY	MONDAY	TUESDAY	WEDNESDAY	THURSDAY	FRIDAY	SATURDAY
DATE:							
7:00 AM							
8:00 AM							
9:00 AM							
10:00 AM							
11:00 AM							
12:00 AM							
1:00 PM							
2:00 PM							
3:00 PM							
4:00 PM							
5:00 PM							
6:00 PM							
7:00 PM							

	SUNDAY	MONDAY	TUESDAY	WEDNESDAY	THURSDAY	FRIDAY	SATURDAY
DATE:							
7:00 AM							
8:00 AM							
9:00 AM							
10:00 AM							
11:00 AM							
12:00 AM							
1:00 PM							
2:00 PM							
3:00 PM							
4:00 PM							
5:00 PM							
6:00 PM							
7:00 PM							

There is just as much horse sense as ever, but the horses have most of it.

	SUNDAY	MONDAY	TUESDAY	WEDNESDAY	THURSDAY	FRIDAY	SATURDAY
DATE:							
7:00 AM							
8:00 AM							
9:00 AM							
10:00 AM							
11:00 AM							
12:00 AM							
1:00 PM							
2:00 PM							
3:00 PM							
4:00 PM							
5:00 PM							
6:00 PM							
7:00 PM							

	SUNDAY	MONDAY	TUESDAY	WEDNESDAY	THURSDAY	FRIDAY	SATURDAY
DATE:							
7:00 AM							
8:00 AM							
9:00 AM							
10:00 AM							
11:00 AM							
12:00 AM							
1:00 PM							
2:00 PM							
3:00 PM							
4:00 PM							
5:00 PM							
6:00 PM							
7:00 PM							

There is nothing so good for the inside of a man as the outside of a horse. ~ John Lubbock

	SUNDAY	MONDAY	TUESDAY	WEDNESDAY	THURSDAY	FRIDAY	SATURDAY
DATE:							
7:00 AM							
8:00 AM							
9:00 AM							
10:00 AM							
11:00 AM							
12:00 AM							
1:00 PM							
2:00 PM							
3:00 PM							
4:00 PM							
5:00 PM							
6:00 PM							
7:00 PM							

	SUNDAY	MONDAY	TUESDAY	WEDNESDAY	THURSDAY	FRIDAY	SATURDAY
DATE:							
7:00 AM							
8:00 AM							
9:00 AM							
10:00 AM							
11:00 AM							
12:00 AM							
1:00 PM							
2:00 PM							
3:00 PM							
4:00 PM							
5:00 PM							
6:00 PM							
7:00 PM							

People on horses look better than they are. People
in cars look worse than they are. ~ Marya Mannes

	SUNDAY	MONDAY	TUESDAY	WEDNESDAY	THURSDAY	FRIDAY	SATURDAY
DATE:							
7:00 AM							
8:00 AM							
9:00 AM							
10:00 AM							
11:00 AM							
12:00 AM							
1:00 PM							
2:00 PM							
3:00 PM							
4:00 PM							
5:00 PM							
6:00 PM							
7:00 PM							

	SUNDAY	MONDAY	TUESDAY	WEDNESDAY	THURSDAY	FRIDAY	SATURDAY
DATE:							
7:00 AM							
8:00 AM							
9:00 AM							
10:00 AM							
11:00 AM							
12:00 AM							
1:00 PM							
2:00 PM							
3:00 PM							
4:00 PM							
5:00 PM							
6:00 PM							
7:00 PM							

To see the wind's power, the rain's cleansing and the
sun's radiant life, one need only to look at the horse.

	SUNDAY	MONDAY	TUESDAY	WEDNESDAY	THURSDAY	FRIDAY	SATURDAY
DATE:							
7:00 AM							
8:00 AM							
9:00 AM							
10:00 AM							
11:00 AM							
12:00 AM							
1:00 PM							
2:00 PM							
3:00 PM							
4:00 PM							
5:00 PM							
6:00 PM							
7:00 PM							

	SUNDAY	MONDAY	TUESDAY	WEDNESDAY	THURSDAY	FRIDAY	SATURDAY
DATE:							
7:00 AM							
8:00 AM							
9:00 AM							
10:00 AM							
11:00 AM							
12:00 AM							
1:00 PM							
2:00 PM							
3:00 PM							
4:00 PM							
5:00 PM							
6:00 PM							
7:00 PM							

To many, the words love, hope and dreams are synonymous with horses.

	SUNDAY	MONDAY	TUESDAY	WEDNESDAY	THURSDAY	FRIDAY	SATURDAY
DATE:							
7:00 AM							
8:00 AM							
9:00 AM							
10:00 AM							
11:00 AM							
12:00 AM							
1:00 PM							
2:00 PM							
3:00 PM							
4:00 PM							
5:00 PM							
6:00 PM							
7:00 PM							

	SUNDAY	MONDAY	TUESDAY	WEDNESDAY	THURSDAY	FRIDAY	SATURDAY
DATE:							
7:00 AM							
8:00 AM							
9:00 AM							
10:00 AM							
11:00 AM							
12:00 AM							
1:00 PM							
2:00 PM							
3:00 PM							
4:00 PM							
5:00 PM							
6:00 PM							
7:00 PM							

The essential joy of being with horses is that it brings us in contact with the rare elements of grace, beauty, spirit and freedom. ~ Sharon Ralls Lemon

DATE:	SUNDAY	MONDAY	TUESDAY	WEDNESDAY	THURSDAY	FRIDAY	SATURDAY
7:00 AM							
8:00 AM							
9:00 AM							
10:00 AM							
11:00 AM							
12:00 AM							
1:00 PM							
2:00 PM							
3:00 PM							
4:00 PM							
5:00 PM							
6:00 PM							
7:00 PM							

	SUNDAY	MONDAY	TUESDAY	WEDNESDAY	THURSDAY	FRIDAY	SATURDAY
DATE:							
7:00 AM							
8:00 AM							
9:00 AM							
10:00 AM							
11:00 AM							
12:00 AM							
1:00 PM							
2:00 PM							
3:00 PM							
4:00 PM							
5:00 PM							
6:00 PM							
7:00 PM							

A horse is like a violin, first it must be tuned, and when tuned it must be accurately played.

	SUNDAY	MONDAY	TUESDAY	WEDNESDAY	THURSDAY	FRIDAY	SATURDAY
DATE:							
7:00 AM							
8:00 AM							
9:00 AM							
10:00 AM							
11:00 AM							
12:00 AM							
1:00 PM							
2:00 PM							
3:00 PM							
4:00 PM							
5:00 PM							
6:00 PM							
7:00 PM							

	SUNDAY	MONDAY	TUESDAY	WEDNESDAY	THURSDAY	FRIDAY	SATURDAY
DATE:							
7:00 AM							
8:00 AM							
9:00 AM							
10:00 AM							
11:00 AM							
12:00 AM							
1:00 PM							
2:00 PM							
3:00 PM							
4:00 PM							
5:00 PM							
6:00 PM							
7:00 PM							

When riding my horse I no longer have my heart in my chest, but between my knees.

	SUNDAY	MONDAY	TUESDAY	WEDNESDAY	THURSDAY	FRIDAY	SATURDAY
DATE:							
7:00 AM							
8:00 AM							
9:00 AM							
10:00 AM							
11:00 AM							
12:00 AM							
1:00 PM							
2:00 PM							
3:00 PM							
4:00 PM							
5:00 PM							
6:00 PM							
7:00 PM							

	SUNDAY	MONDAY	TUESDAY	WEDNESDAY	THURSDAY	FRIDAY	SATURDAY
DATE:							
7:00 AM							
8:00 AM							
9:00 AM							
10:00 AM							
11:00 AM							
12:00 AM							
1:00 PM							
2:00 PM							
3:00 PM							
4:00 PM							
5:00 PM							
6:00 PM							
7:00 PM							

I've spent most of my life riding horses. The rest I've just wasted.

	SUNDAY	MONDAY	TUESDAY	WEDNESDAY	THURSDAY	FRIDAY	SATURDAY
DATE:							
7:00 AM							
8:00 AM							
9:00 AM							
10:00 AM							
11:00 AM							
12:00 AM							
1:00 PM							
2:00 PM							
3:00 PM							
4:00 PM							
5:00 PM							
6:00 PM							
7:00 PM							

	SUNDAY	MONDAY	TUESDAY	WEDNESDAY	THURSDAY	FRIDAY	SATURDAY
DATE:							
7:00 AM							
8:00 AM							
9:00 AM							
10:00 AM							
11:00 AM							
12:00 AM							
1:00 PM							
2:00 PM							
3:00 PM							
4:00 PM							
5:00 PM							
6:00 PM							
7:00 PM							

**A stubborn horse walks behind you, an impatient horse walks
in front of you, but a noble companion walks beside you.**

	SUNDAY	MONDAY	TUESDAY	WEDNESDAY	THURSDAY	FRIDAY	SATURDAY
DATE:							
7:00 AM							
8:00 AM							
9:00 AM							
10:00 AM							
11:00 AM							
12:00 AM							
1:00 PM							
2:00 PM							
3:00 PM							
4:00 PM							
5:00 PM							
6:00 PM							
7:00 PM							

	SUNDAY	MONDAY	TUESDAY	WEDNESDAY	THURSDAY	FRIDAY	SATURDAY
DATE:							
7:00 AM							
8:00 AM							
9:00 AM							
10:00 AM							
11:00 AM							
12:00 AM							
1:00 PM							
2:00 PM							
3:00 PM							
4:00 PM							
5:00 PM							
6:00 PM							
7:00 PM							

If a horse stands on you its because you're in the way.

	SUNDAY	MONDAY	TUESDAY	WEDNESDAY	THURSDAY	FRIDAY	SATURDAY
DATE:							
7:00 AM							
8:00 AM							
9:00 AM							
10:00 AM							
11:00 AM							
12:00 AM							
1:00 PM							
2:00 PM							
3:00 PM							
4:00 PM							
5:00 PM							
6:00 PM							
7:00 PM							

	SUNDAY	MONDAY	TUESDAY	WEDNESDAY	THURSDAY	FRIDAY	SATURDAY
DATE:							
7:00 AM							
8:00 AM							
9:00 AM							
10:00 AM							
11:00 AM							
12:00 AM							
1:00 PM							
2:00 PM							
3:00 PM							
4:00 PM							
5:00 PM							
6:00 PM							
7:00 PM							

Grooming: the process by which the dirt on the horse is transferred to the groom.

	SUNDAY	MONDAY	TUESDAY	WEDNESDAY	THURSDAY	FRIDAY	SATURDAY
DATE:							
7:00 AM							
8:00 AM							
9:00 AM							
10:00 AM							
11:00 AM							
12:00 AM							
1:00 PM							
2:00 PM							
3:00 PM							
4:00 PM							
5:00 PM							
6:00 PM							
7:00 PM							

	SUNDAY	MONDAY	TUESDAY	WEDNESDAY	THURSDAY	FRIDAY	SATURDAY
DATE:							
7:00 AM							
8:00 AM							
9:00 AM							
10:00 AM							
11:00 AM							
12:00 AM							
1:00 PM							
2:00 PM							
3:00 PM							
4:00 PM							
5:00 PM							
6:00 PM							
7:00 PM							

The love for a horse is just as complicated as the love for another human being...If you never love a horse, you will never understand.

	SUNDAY	MONDAY	TUESDAY	WEDNESDAY	THURSDAY	FRIDAY	SATURDAY
DATE:							
7:00 AM							
8:00 AM							
9:00 AM							
10:00 AM							
11:00 AM							
12:00 AM							
1:00 PM							
2:00 PM							
3:00 PM							
4:00 PM							
5:00 PM							
6:00 PM							
7:00 PM							

	SUNDAY	MONDAY	TUESDAY	WEDNESDAY	THURSDAY	FRIDAY	SATURDAY
DATE:							
7:00 AM							
8:00 AM							
9:00 AM							
10:00 AM							
11:00 AM							
12:00 AM							
1:00 PM							
2:00 PM							
3:00 PM							
4:00 PM							
5:00 PM							
6:00 PM							
7:00 PM							

Of all creatures God made at the Creation, there is none more
excellent, or so much to be respected as a horse. – Bedouin Legend

	SUNDAY	MONDAY	TUESDAY	WEDNESDAY	THURSDAY	FRIDAY	SATURDAY
DATE:							
7:00 AM							
8:00 AM							
9:00 AM							
10:00 AM							
11:00 AM							
12:00 AM							
1:00 PM							
2:00 PM							
3:00 PM							
4:00 PM							
5:00 PM							
6:00 PM							
7:00 PM							

	SUNDAY	MONDAY	TUESDAY	WEDNESDAY	THURSDAY	FRIDAY	SATURDAY
DATE:							
7:00 AM							
8:00 AM							
9:00 AM							
10:00 AM							
11:00 AM							
12:00 AM							
1:00 PM							
2:00 PM							
3:00 PM							
4:00 PM							
5:00 PM							
6:00 PM							
7:00 PM							

I whisper to my horse, but he never listens!

	SUNDAY	MONDAY	TUESDAY	WEDNESDAY	THURSDAY	FRIDAY	SATURDAY
DATE:							
7:00 AM							
8:00 AM							
9:00 AM							
10:00 AM							
11:00 AM							
12:00 AM							
1:00 PM							
2:00 PM							
3:00 PM							
4:00 PM							
5:00 PM							
6:00 PM							
7:00 PM							

	SUNDAY	MONDAY	TUESDAY	WEDNESDAY	THURSDAY	FRIDAY	SATURDAY
DATE:							
7:00 AM							
8:00 AM							
9:00 AM							
10:00 AM							
11:00 AM							
12:00 AM							
1:00 PM							
2:00 PM							
3:00 PM							
4:00 PM							
5:00 PM							
6:00 PM							
7:00 PM							

The horse. Here is nobility without conceit, friendship without
45envy, beauty without vanity. A willing servant, yet never a slave.

	SUNDAY	MONDAY	TUESDAY	WEDNESDAY	THURSDAY	FRIDAY	SATURDAY
DATE:							
7:00 AM							
8:00 AM							
9:00 AM							
10:00 AM							
11:00 AM							
12:00 AM							
1:00 PM							
2:00 PM							
3:00 PM							
4:00 PM							
5:00 PM							
6:00 PM							
7:00 PM							

	SUNDAY	MONDAY	TUESDAY	WEDNESDAY	THURSDAY	FRIDAY	SATURDAY
DATE:							
7:00 AM							
8:00 AM							
9:00 AM							
10:00 AM							
11:00 AM							
12:00 AM							
1:00 PM							
2:00 PM							
3:00 PM							
4:00 PM							
5:00 PM							
6:00 PM							
7:00 PM							

No matter how bad your day is there is always someone waiting for you at the barn.

	SUNDAY	MONDAY	TUESDAY	WEDNESDAY	THURSDAY	FRIDAY	SATURDAY
DATE:							
7:00 AM							
8:00 AM							
9:00 AM							
10:00 AM							
11:00 AM							
12:00 AM							
1:00 PM							
2:00 PM							
3:00 PM							
4:00 PM							
5:00 PM							
6:00 PM							
7:00 PM							

	SUNDAY	MONDAY	TUESDAY	WEDNESDAY	THURSDAY	FRIDAY	SATURDAY
DATE:							
7:00 AM							
8:00 AM							
9:00 AM							
10:00 AM							
11:00 AM							
12:00 AM							
1:00 PM							
2:00 PM							
3:00 PM							
4:00 PM							
5:00 PM							
6:00 PM							
7:00 PM							

A horse is your best friend. You can tell them anything and no one else will ever know.

	SUNDAY	MONDAY	TUESDAY	WEDNESDAY	THURSDAY	FRIDAY	SATURDAY
DATE:							
7:00 AM							
8:00 AM							
9:00 AM							
10:00 AM							
11:00 AM							
12:00 AM							
1:00 PM							
2:00 PM							
3:00 PM							
4:00 PM							
5:00 PM							
6:00 PM							
7:00 PM							

	SUNDAY	MONDAY	TUESDAY	WEDNESDAY	THURSDAY	FRIDAY	SATURDAY
DATE:							
7:00 AM							
8:00 AM							
9:00 AM							
10:00 AM							
11:00 AM							
12:00 AM							
1:00 PM							
2:00 PM							
3:00 PM							
4:00 PM							
5:00 PM							
6:00 PM							
7:00 PM							

Whoever said a horse was dumb, was dumb. ~ Will Rogers

	SUNDAY	MONDAY	TUESDAY	WEDNESDAY	THURSDAY	FRIDAY	SATURDAY
DATE:							
7:00 AM							
8:00 AM							
9:00 AM							
10:00 AM							
11:00 AM							
12:00 AM							
1:00 PM							
2:00 PM							
3:00 PM							
4:00 PM							
5:00 PM							
6:00 PM							
7:00 PM							

	SUNDAY	MONDAY	TUESDAY	WEDNESDAY	THURSDAY	FRIDAY	SATURDAY
DATE:							
7:00 AM							
8:00 AM							
9:00 AM							
10:00 AM							
11:00 AM							
12:00 AM							
1:00 PM							
2:00 PM							
3:00 PM							
4:00 PM							
5:00 PM							
6:00 PM							
7:00 PM							

He knows when you're happy. He knows when you're comfortable. He knows when you're confident. And he always knows when you have carrots.

	SUNDAY	MONDAY	TUESDAY	WEDNESDAY	THURSDAY	FRIDAY	SATURDAY
DATE:							
7:00 AM							
8:00 AM							
9:00 AM							
10:00 AM							
11:00 AM							
12:00 AM							
1:00 PM							
2:00 PM							
3:00 PM							
4:00 PM							
5:00 PM							
6:00 PM							
7:00 PM							

	SUNDAY	MONDAY	TUESDAY	WEDNESDAY	THURSDAY	FRIDAY	SATURDAY
DATE:							
7:00 AM							
8:00 AM							
9:00 AM							
10:00 AM							
11:00 AM							
12:00 AM							
1:00 PM							
2:00 PM							
3:00 PM							
4:00 PM							
5:00 PM							
6:00 PM							
7:00 PM							

Through the days of love and celebration and joy, and through the dark days of mourning — the faithful horse has been with us always. ~ Elizabeth Cotton

	SUNDAY	MONDAY	TUESDAY	WEDNESDAY	THURSDAY	FRIDAY	SATURDAY
DATE:							
7:00 AM							
8:00 AM							
9:00 AM							
10:00 AM							
11:00 AM							
12:00 AM							
1:00 PM							
2:00 PM							
3:00 PM							
4:00 PM							
5:00 PM							
6:00 PM							
7:00 PM							

	SUNDAY	MONDAY	TUESDAY	WEDNESDAY	THURSDAY	FRIDAY	SATURDAY
DATE:							
7:00 AM							
8:00 AM							
9:00 AM							
10:00 AM							
11:00 AM							
12:00 AM							
1:00 PM							
2:00 PM							
3:00 PM							
4:00 PM							
5:00 PM							
6:00 PM							
7:00 PM							

The history of humankind is carried on the back of a horse.

	SUNDAY	MONDAY	TUESDAY	WEDNESDAY	THURSDAY	FRIDAY	SATURDAY
DATE:							
7:00 AM							
8:00 AM							
9:00 AM							
10:00 AM							
11:00 AM							
12:00 AM							
1:00 PM							
2:00 PM							
3:00 PM							
4:00 PM							
5:00 PM							
6:00 PM							
7:00 PM							

	SUNDAY	MONDAY	TUESDAY	WEDNESDAY	THURSDAY	FRIDAY	SATURDAY
DATE:							
7:00 AM							
8:00 AM							
9:00 AM							
10:00 AM							
11:00 AM							
12:00 AM							
1:00 PM							
2:00 PM							
3:00 PM							
4:00 PM							
5:00 PM							
6:00 PM							
7:00 PM							

I heard a neigh. Oh, such a brisk and melodious neigh it was.
My very heart leapt with the sound. ~ Nathaniel Hawthorne

	SUNDAY	MONDAY	TUESDAY	WEDNESDAY	THURSDAY	FRIDAY	SATURDAY
DATE:							
7:00 AM							
8:00 AM							
9:00 AM							
10:00 AM							
11:00 AM							
12:00 AM							
1:00 PM							
2:00 PM							
3:00 PM							
4:00 PM							
5:00 PM							
6:00 PM							
7:00 PM							

	SUNDAY	MONDAY	TUESDAY	WEDNESDAY	THURSDAY	FRIDAY	SATURDAY
DATE:							
7:00 AM							
8:00 AM							
9:00 AM							
10:00 AM							
11:00 AM							
12:00 AM							
1:00 PM							
2:00 PM							
3:00 PM							
4:00 PM							
5:00 PM							
6:00 PM							
7:00 PM							

If your horse says 'no,' you either asked the wrong
question, or asked the question wrong. ~ Pat Parelli

	SUNDAY	MONDAY	TUESDAY	WEDNESDAY	THURSDAY	FRIDAY	SATURDAY
DATE:							
7:00 AM							
8:00 AM							
9:00 AM							
10:00 AM							
11:00 AM							
12:00 AM							
1:00 PM							
2:00 PM							
3:00 PM							
4:00 PM							
5:00 PM							
6:00 PM							
7:00 PM							

	SUNDAY	MONDAY	TUESDAY	WEDNESDAY	THURSDAY	FRIDAY	SATURDAY
DATE:							
7:00 AM							
8:00 AM							
9:00 AM							
10:00 AM							
11:00 AM							
12:00 AM							
1:00 PM							
2:00 PM							
3:00 PM							
4:00 PM							
5:00 PM							
6:00 PM							
7:00 PM							

No philosophers so thoroughly comprehend us as dogs and horses. ~ Herman Melville

	SUNDAY	MONDAY	TUESDAY	WEDNESDAY	THURSDAY	FRIDAY	SATURDAY
DATE:							
7:00 AM							
8:00 AM							
9:00 AM							
10:00 AM							
11:00 AM							
12:00 AM							
1:00 PM							
2:00 PM							
3:00 PM							
4:00 PM							
5:00 PM							
6:00 PM							
7:00 PM							

	SUNDAY	MONDAY	TUESDAY	WEDNESDAY	THURSDAY	FRIDAY	SATURDAY
DATE:							
7:00 AM							
8:00 AM							
9:00 AM							
10:00 AM							
11:00 AM							
12:00 AM							
1:00 PM							
2:00 PM							
3:00 PM							
4:00 PM							
5:00 PM							
6:00 PM							
7:00 PM							

In riding a horse, we borrow freedom. ~ Helen Thompson

	SUNDAY	MONDAY	TUESDAY	WEDNESDAY	THURSDAY	FRIDAY	SATURDAY
DATE:							
7:00 AM							
8:00 AM							
9:00 AM							
10:00 AM							
11:00 AM							
12:00 AM							
1:00 PM							
2:00 PM							
3:00 PM							
4:00 PM							
5:00 PM							
6:00 PM							
7:00 PM							

	SUNDAY	MONDAY	TUESDAY	WEDNESDAY	THURSDAY	FRIDAY	SATURDAY
DATE:							
7:00 AM							
8:00 AM							
9:00 AM							
10:00 AM							
11:00 AM							
12:00 AM							
1:00 PM							
2:00 PM							
3:00 PM							
4:00 PM							
5:00 PM							
6:00 PM							
7:00 PM							

When you are on a great horse, you have the best
seat you will ever have. ~ Sir Winston Churchill

	SUNDAY	MONDAY	TUESDAY	WEDNESDAY	THURSDAY	FRIDAY	SATURDAY
DATE:							
7:00 AM							
8:00 AM							
9:00 AM							
10:00 AM							
11:00 AM							
12:00 AM							
1:00 PM							
2:00 PM							
3:00 PM							
4:00 PM							
5:00 PM							
6:00 PM							
7:00 PM							

NOTES

When people say it's JUST a horse,
they JUST don't understand...

Made in the USA
Las Vegas, NV
07 September 2022

54865670R00208